PLOTINUS

ENNEAD V.8

THE *ENNEADS* OF PLOTINUS

With Philosophical Commentaries

Series Editors: John M. Dillon, Trinity College, Dublin and Andrew Smith, University College, Dublin

Also Available in the Series:

I.1: *What Is the Living Thing? What Is Man?* by Gerard O'Daly
I.6: *On Beauty* by Andrew Smith
II.5: *On What Is Potentially and What Actually* by Cinzia Arruzza
II.9: *Against the Gnostics* by Sebastian Ramon Philipp Gertz
IV.3–4.29: *Problems Concerning the Soul* by John M. Dillon & H. J. Blumenthal
IV.4.30–45 & IV.5: *Problems Concerning the Soul* by Gary Gurtler
IV.7: *On the Immortality of the Soul* by Barrie Fleet
IV.8: *On the Descent of the Soul Into Bodies* by Barrie Fleet
V.1: *On the Three Primary Levels of Reality* by Eric D. Perl
V.5: *That the Intelligibles are not External to Intellect, and on the Good* by Lloyd P. Gerson
VI.4 & VI.5: *On the Presence of Being, One and the Same, Everywhere as a Whole* by Eyjólfur Emilsson & Steven Strange
VI.8: *On the Voluntary and on the Free Will of the One* by Kevin Corrigan and John D. Turner

Forthcoming Titles in the Series Include:

I.2: *On Virtues* by Suzanne Stern-Gillet
I.3: *On Dialectic* by Pauliina Remes
I.4: *On Well-Being* by Kieran McGroarty
I.5: *On Whether Well Being Increases With Time* by Danielle A. Layne
I.8: *On the Nature and Source of Evil* by Anne Sheppard
II.4: *On Matter* by Anthony A. Long
II.7: *On Complete Blending* by Robert Goulding
II.8: *On Sight* by Robert Goulding
III.4: *On Our Allotted Guardian Spirit* by Wiebke-Marie Stock
III.5: *On Love* by Sara Magrin
III.6: *On Impassibility* by Eleni Perdikouri
III.7: *On Eternity and Time* by László Bene
III.8: *On Nature and Contemplation* by George Karamanolis
IV.6: *On Sense-Perception and Memory* by Peter Lautner
V.2, **V.4**, and **V.6**: *On the One and Intellect* by Eleni Perdikouri
V.3: *On the Knowing Hypostases* by Marie-Élise Zovko
V.9: *On Intellect, Ideas, and Being* by Matthias Vorwerk
VI.1–2: *On the Genera of Being (I+II)* by Damien Caluori & Regina Füchslin
VI.3: *On the Genera of Being (III)* by Riccardo Chiaradonna
VI.7: *The Forms and the Good* by Nicholas Banner
VI.9: *On the Good or the One* by Stephen R. L. Clark

PLOTINUS
ENNEAD V.8

On Intelligible Beauty

Translation with an Introduction
and Commentary

ANDREW SMITH

PARMENIDES
PUBLISHING
Las Vegas | Zurich | Athens

PARMENIDES PUBLISHING
Las Vegas | Zurich | Athens

This edition published in 2017 by Parmenides Publishing
in the United States of America

ISBN soft cover: 978-1-930972-65-0
ISBN ebook: 978-1-930972-97-1

Library of Congress Cataloging-in-Publication Data

Names: Plotinus, author. | Smith, Andrew, 1945- translator, commentator.
Title: Ennead V.8 : on intelligible beauty / Plotinus ; translation with an introduction and commentary, Andrew Smith.
Other titles: Ennead. V, 8. English | On intelligible beauty
Description: 1st edition. | Las Vegas, NV : Parmenides Publishing, 2017. | Series: The Enneads of Plotinus with philosophical commentaries | Includes bibliographical references and index.
Identifiers: LCCN 2017036265| ISBN 9781930972650 (pbk. : alk. paper) | ISBN 9781930972971 (ebook)
Subjects: LCSH: Plotinus. Ennead. V, 8. | Aesthetics, Ancient--Early works to 1800.
Classification: LCC B693.E52 E5 2017d | DDC 186/.4--dc23
LC record available at https://lccn.loc.gov/2017036265

Typeset in Warnock and Futura by Parmenides Publishing
Printed by Edwards Brothers Malloy, Chicago, IL
www.edwardsbrothersmalloy.com

www.parmenides.com

For Freya

Contents

Introduction to the Series 1

Abbreviations 11

Acknowledgements 15

INTRODUCTION TO THE TREATISE 17

Note on the Greek Text 31

Synopsis 33

TRANSLATION 43

COMMENTARY 69

- Chapter 1 69
- Chapter 2 77
- Chapter 3 83
- Chapter 4 91
- Chapter 5 99
- Chapter 6 105
- Chapter 7 109
- Chapter 8 117
- Chapter 9 119

Chapter 10 125
Chapter 11 131
Chapter 12 135
Chapter 13 139

Select Bibliography 143
Index of Ancient Authors 153
Index of Names and Subjects 159

Introduction to the Series With a Brief Outline of the Life and Thought of Plotinus (205–270 CE)

PLOTINUS WAS BORN IN 205 CE in Egypt of Greek-speaking parents. He attended the philosophical schools in Alexandria where he would have studied Plato (427–347 BCE), Aristotle (384–322 BCE), the Stoics and Epicureans as well as other Greek philosophical traditions. He began his serious philosophical education, however, relatively late in life, at the age of twenty-seven and was deeply impressed by the Platonist Ammonius Saccas about whom we, unfortunately, know very little, but with whom Plotinus studied for some eleven years. Even our knowledge of Plotinus' life is limited to what we can glean from Porphyry's introduction to his edition of his philosophical treatises, an account colored by Porphyry's own concerns. After completing his studies in Alexandria Plotinus attempted, by joining a military expedition of the Roman emperor Gordian III, to make contact with the

Brahmins in order to learn something of Indian thought. Unfortunately Gordian was defeated and killed (244). Plotinus somehow managed to extract himself and we next hear of him in Rome where he was able to set up a school of philosophy in the house of a high-ranking Roman lady by the name of Gemina. It is, perhaps, surprising that he had no formal contacts with the Platonic Academy in Athens, which was headed at the time by Longinus, but Longinus was familiar with his work, partly at least through Porphyry who had studied in Athens. The fact that it was Rome where Plotinus set up his school may be due to the originality of his philosophical activity and to his patrons. He clearly had some influential contacts, not least with the philhellenic emperor Gallienus (253–268), who may also have encouraged his later failed attempt to set up a civic community based on Platonic principles in a ruined city in Campania.

Plotinus' school was, like most ancient schools of philosophy, relatively small in scale, but did attract distinguished students from abroad and from the Roman upper classes. It included not only philosophers but also politicians and members of the medical profession who wished to lead the philosophical life. His most famous student was Porphyry (233–305) who, as a relative latecomer to the school, persuaded him to put into writing the results of his seminars. It is almost certain that we possess most, if not all, of his written output, which represents his mature thought, since he didn't commence writing until the age of forty-eight. The school seemingly had inner and outer circles, and Plotinus himself was clearly an inspiring and sympathetic teacher who took a deep interest in the philosophical and spiritual progress of his students. Porphyry tells us that when he was suffering from severe depression Plotinus straight away visited him in his lodgings to help him. His concern for others is also illustrated by the fact that he was entrusted with the personal education of many orphans and the care of their property and careers. The reconciliation of this worldly involvement with the encouragement to lead a life of contemplation is encapsulated in Porphyry's comment that "he was present to himself and others at the same time."

The *Enneads* of Plotinus is the edition of his treatises arranged by his pupil Porphyry who tried to put shape to the collection he had inherited by organizing it into six sets of nine treatises (hence the name *"Enneads")* that led the reader through the levels of Plotinus' universe, from the physical world to Soul, Intellect and, finally, to the highest principle, the One. Although Plotinus undoubtedly had a clearly structured metaphysical system by the time he began committing himself to expressing his thought in written form, the treatises themselves are not systematic expositions, but rather explorations of particular themes and issues raised in interpreting Plato and other philosophical texts read in the School. In fact, to achieve his neat arrangement Porphyry was sometimes driven even to dividing certain treatises (e.g., III.2–3; IV.3–5, and VI.4–5).

Although Plotinus' writings are not transcripts of his seminars, but are directed to the reader, they do, nevertheless, convey the sort of lively debate that he encouraged in his school. Frequently he takes for granted that a particular set of ideas is already familiar as having been treated in an earlier seminar that may or may not be found in the written text. For this reason it is useful for the reader to have some idea of the main philosophical principles of his system as they can be extracted from the *Enneads* as a whole.

Plotinus regarded himself as a faithful interpreter of Plato whose thought lies at the core of his entire project. But Plato's thought, whilst definitive, does according to Plotinus require careful exposition and clarification, often in the light of other thinkers such as Aristotle and the Stoics. It is because of this creative application of different traditions of ancient thought to the interpretation of Plato that Plotinus' version of Platonism became, partly through the medium of later Platonists such as Porphyry, Iamblichus (245–325), and Proclus (412–485), an influential source and way of reading both Plato and Aristotle in the Middle Ages, the Renaissance, and up to the early 19th century, when scholars first began to differentiate Plato and "Neoplatonism." His thought, too, provided early Christian theologians of the Latin and particularly of the Byzantine tradition, with a rich variety of metaphysical concepts with which to explore and express difficult doctrinal ideas. His fashioning of Plato's ideas into a consistent metaphysical structure, though no longer accepted as a uniquely valid way of approaching Plato, was influential in promoting the notion of metaphysical systems in early modern philosophy. More recently increasing interest has centered on his exploration of the self, levels of consciousness, and his expansion of discourse beyond the levels of normal ontology to the examination of what lies both above and beneath being. His thought continues to challenge us when confronted with the issue of man's nature and role in the universe and of the extent and limitations of human knowledge.

Whilst much of Plotinus' metaphysical structure is recognizably an interpretation of Plato it is an interpretation that is not always immediately obvious just because it is filtered through several centuries of developing Platonic thought, itself already overlaid with important concepts drawn from other schools. It is, nevertheless, useful as a starting point to see how Plotinus attempts to bring coherence to what he believed to be a comprehensive worldview expressed in the Platonic dialogues. The Platonic Forms are central. They become for him an intelligible universe that is the source and model of the physical universe. But aware of Aristotle's criticism of the Platonic Forms as lifeless causes he takes on board Aristotle's concept of god as a self-thinker to enable him to identify this intelligible universe as a divine Intellect that thinks itself as the Forms or Intelligibles. The doctrine of the Forms as the thoughts of god had already entered Platonism, but not as the rigorously argued identity that Plotinus proposed. Moreover the Intelligibles, since they are identical with Intellect, are themselves actively intellectual; they are intellects. Thus Plato's world of Forms has become a complex and dynamic intelligible universe in which unity and plurality, stability, and activity are reconciled.

Now although the divine Intellect is one it also embraces plurality, both because its thoughts, the Intelligibles, are many and because it may itself be analyzed into thinker and thought. Its unity demands a further principle, which is the cause of its unity. This principle, which is the cause of all unity and being but does not possess unity or being in itself, he calls the One, an interpretation of the Idea of the Good in Plato's *Republic* that is "beyond being" and that may be seen as the simple (hence "one") source of all reality. We thus have the first two of what subsequently became known as the three Hypostases, the One, Intellect, and Soul, the last of which acts as an intermediary between the intelligible and physical universes. This last Hypostasis takes on all the functions of transmitting form and life that may be found in Plato, although Plato himself does not always make such a clear distinction between soul and intellect. Thus the One is the ultimate source of all, including this universe, which is then prefigured in Intellect and transmitted through Soul to become manifest as our physical universe. Matter, which receives imperfectly this expression, is conceived not as an independently existing counter-principle, a dangerously dualist notion, but is in a sense itself a product of the One, a kind of non-being that, while being nothing specific in itself, nevertheless is not simply not there.

But this procession from an ultimate principle is balanced by a return movement at each level of reality that fully constitutes itself only when it turns back in contemplation of its producer. And so the whole of reality is a dynamic movement of procession and return, except for matter, which has no life of its own to make this return; it is inert. This movement of return, which may be traced back to the force of "love" in Plato or Aristotle's final cause, is characterized by Plotinus as a cognitive activity, a form of contemplation, weaker at each successive level, from Intellect through discursive reasoning to the merest image of rational order as expressed in the objects of the physical universe.

The human individual mirrors this structure to which we are all related at each level. For each of us has a body and soul, an intellect, and even something within us that relates to the One. While it is the nature of soul to give life to body, the higher aspect of our soul also has aspirations toward intellect, the true self, and even beyond. This urge to return corresponds to the cosmic movement of return. But the tension between soul's natural duty to body and its origins in the intelligible can be, for the individual, a source of fracture and alienation in which the soul becomes over-involved and overwhelmed by the body and so estranged from its true self. Plotinus encourages us to make the return or ascent, but at the same time attempts to resolve the conflict of duties by reconciling the two-fold nature of soul as life-giving and contemplative.

This is the general framework within which important traditional philosophical issues are encountered, discussed and resolved, but always in a spirit of inquiry and ongoing debate. Issues are frequently encountered in several different contexts, each angle providing a different insight. The nature of the soul and its relationship to the body is examined at length (IV) using the Aristotelian distinctions of levels of soul (vegetative, growth, sensitive, rational) whilst maintaining the immortal nature of the transcendent soul in Platonic terms. The active nature of the soul in sense-perception is maintained to preserve the principle that incorporeals cannot be affected by corporeal reality. A vigorous discussion (VI.4 and 5) on the general nature of the relationship of incorporeals to body explores in every detail and in great depth the way in which incorporeals act on body. A universe that is the product of design is reconciled with the freedom of the individual. And, not least, the time-bound nature of the physical universe and human reason is grounded in the life of Intellect, which subsists in eternity. Sometimes, however, Plotinus seems to break outside the framework of traditional metaphysics: the nature of matter and the One, each as non-being, though in a different sense, strains the terminology and structure of traditional ontology; and the attempt to reconcile the role of the individual soul within the traditional Platonic distinction of transcendent and immanent reality leads to a novel exploration of the nature of the self, the "I."

It is this restless urge for exploration and inquiry that lends to the treatises of Plotinus their philosophical vitality. Whilst presenting us with a rich and complexly coherent system, he constantly engages us in philosophical inquiry. In this way each treatise presents us with new ideas and fresh challenges. And, for Plotinus, every philosophical engagement is not just a mental exercise but also contributes to the rediscovery of the self and our reintegration with the source of all being, the Platonic aim of "becoming like god."

While Plotinus, like Plato, always wishes to engage his audience to reflect for themselves, his treatises are not easy reading, partly no doubt because his own audience was already familiar with many of his basic ideas and, more importantly, had been exposed in his seminars to critical readings of philosophical texts that have not survived to our day. Another problem is that the treatises do not lay out his thought in a systematic way but take up specific issues, although always the whole system may be discerned in the background. Sometimes, too, the exact flow of thought is difficult to follow because of an often condensed mode of expression.

Because we are convinced that Plotinus has something to say to us today, we have launched this series of translations and commentaries as a means of opening up the text to readers with an interest in grappling with the philosophical issues revealed by an encounter with Plotinus' own words and arguments. Each volume will contain a new translation, careful summaries of the arguments and structure of the treatise, and a philosophical commentary that will aim to throw light on the philosophical meaning and import of the text.

John M. Dillon
Andrew Smith

Abbreviations

Armstrong Armstrong, A. H. 1966–1988. *Plotinus.* Greek Text with English Translation and Introductions. 7 vols. Loeb Classical Library. Cambridge, MA: Harvard University Press. Revised edition of vol. I, 1989.

Aubry Aubry, G. 2004. *Plotin: Traité 53 (I, 1).* Introduction, Translation, Commentary, and Notes. Paris: Cerf.

Denniston Denniston, J. D. 1954. *The Greek Particles.* 2nd edition. Oxford: Clarendon Press.

DK Diels-Kranz. *Die Fragmente der Vorsokratiker.* 6th ed. Berlin: Weidmann, 1961.

Goodwin Goodwin, W. W. 1889. *Syntax of the Moods and Tenses of the Greek Verb.* London: Macmillan.

HBT Harder, R., R. Beutler, and W. Theiler. 1956–1971. *Plotins Schriften.* Greek Text with German Translation and Commentary. 12 vols. Hamburg: Meiner.

HS_1 Henry, P. and –Schwyzer. 1951–1973. *Plotini Opera* I–III (editio maior). Paris: Desclée de Brouwer et Cie.

HS_2 Henry, P. and -Schwyzer. 1964–1982. *Plotini Opera* I–III (editio minor, with revised text). Oxford: Clarendon Press. Where HS_1 and HS_2 agree, HS indicates this.

KRS Kirk, G. S., J. E. Raven, and M. Schofield. 1983. *The Presocratic Philosophers.* 2nd edition. Cambridge: Cambridge University Press.

LS Long, A. A. and D. N. Sedley. 1987. *The Hellenistic Philosophers, Volume 1: Translation of the Principal Sources, with Philosophical Commentary.* Cambridge: Cambridge University Press.

LSJ Liddell, H. G. and R. Scott, eds. *A Greek–English Lexicon.* 1940. 9th edition, revised by H. S. Jones. Oxford: Clarendon Press.

SP	Sleeman, J. H. and G. Pollet. 1980. *Lexicon Plotinianum*. Leiden: Brill and Leuven: Leuven University Press.
SVF	Von Arnim, H., ed.1905–1924. *Stoicorum Veterum Fragmenta*. Leipzig: Teubner.
Tornau	Tornau, C. 2011. *Plotin: Ausgewählte Schriften*. Translation and Commentary. Stuttgart: Reclam.
VP	*Vita Plotini* = Porphyry's *Life of Plotinus*, included in HS_1, HS_2, and in the translations of MacKenna and Armstrong.

Acknowledgments

THE AUTHOR WOULD LIKE TO THANK his co-editor, John Dillon, for helpful remarks on a draft of this work, his wife, Joan, for reading through the manuscript, and, not least, Eliza Tutellier, Sara Hermann, and Gale Carr for their editorial support in the production of this volume and of the series as a whole.

Introduction to the Treatise

ALTHOUGH THIS TREATISE MAY BE READ as an independent piece, as it is presented in modern editions of the *Enneads*, it is also important to place it in its original context as the second section of a long treatise which Porphyry divided into four separate treatises to fit into his enneadic schema[1] of organizing Plotinus' work (III.8, V.8, V.5, II.9). Porphyry's treatment makes a certain sense, in that V.8, like V.5, concentrates on the level of reality represented by Plotinus' intelligible world and so may be fitted into his pattern of treatises in "ascending" metaphysical ranking from the physical world (I–III) to the world of Soul (IV), Intellect (V) and finally the One (VI). But placing it back into its original context helps us to understand not only the rather abrupt statements at the beginning and end of these separated treatises, but to appreciate more clearly the concerns which most engaged Plotinus' attention and colored his presentation during the

1 See page 3.

period of composition. Most noteworthy of these is the final part (II.9) of the original whole treatise with its severe criticism of Gnosticism, a criticism which is grounded in the positive presentation of the metaphysical structure of the universe that occupies much of the preceding parts.

Nevertheless, the way in which Porphyry divided the original treatise does at least mark the breaks between distinct topics, which follow on from each other in a way that makes sense in the context of a criticism of Gnostic beliefs. Thus III.8 *On Contemplation* presents an account of the dynamic power of the entire range of levels of existence understood as forms of cognitive activity or contemplation, ranging from the supreme activity of Intellect to the most fundamental structural principles of the physical universe. This theory is the foundation for an assessment of the physical universe as ultimately dependent on and taking its positive value from the transcendent world of Intellect and ultimately from the One itself, an idea that radically undermines the Gnostic devaluing of the world. The following section, V.8 *On Intelligible Beauty*, examines more closely the transcendent source of the beauty of our universe and its accessibility to us. In V.5 *That the Intelligibles are not External to the Intellect and on the Good*, he analyzes Intellect from an epistemological perspective, before concluding in II.9 *Against the Gnostics* with more specific criticisms of Gnostic metaphysics.

A particular, and perhaps for many modern readers surprising, feature of V.8 is the extensive employment of myth, in this case Hesiod's description of the genealogy of the gods in his *Theogony.* Plotinus is selective and restricts the Hesiodic genealogy to the sequence of three deities: Ouranos as the father of Kronos, and Kronos as father of Zeus. Their mutual relationships are used by him to illustrate the relationship of the One, Intellect, and Soul and, as explained in the commentary, reference to this myth occurs at key points in the first three parts of the original whole treatise, again confirming their close thematic ties. The particular prominence of such allegorical interpretation may have been occasioned partly by Plotinus' concern to engage the attention of those members of his own seminars who had Gnostic leanings,[2] since the Gnostic writings make much use of traditional mythology. Indeed the remark at the beginning of the treatise that it is addressed "to ourselves' (1, 4–5) is a clear indication that any anti-gnostic sentiment expressed in it is intended as a warning for his own students rather than as a general polemic aimed at Gnostics at large.

Although Plotinus' original long treatise can, then, be viewed on the whole as an anti-gnostic warning to his own followers, it deals at the same time with central topics of much wider philosophical concern: for example,

2 See *Life of Plotinus* 16.

the understanding of causality, especially in terms of the relationship of "thinking" or "contemplation" to what is produced by contemplation (III.8), the nature of the intelligible universe and its relationship to this world, the nature and role of the Platonic demiurge (V.8), and the identity of thinker and object of thought in true thinking (V.5). These are issues of concern quite independent of any engagement with Gnosticism.

We have already mentioned the role of myth in V.8 and its companion treatises, a feature which is particularly striking in the final chapters of V.8. Now there has been a tendency by modern scholars to underplay the significance of Plotinus' use of mythology by differentiating him from subsequent Neoplatonists such as Iamblichus, Proclus, and even Porphyry himself, who were more concerned to integrate their philosophizing with the worldviews presented by Greek traditional theology, mythology, and religious practice. But while it is probably the case that Plotinus was far less concerned to accommodate these cultural strands within his own metaphysical system, his employment of them suggests that he certainly did not despise them and even considered them to have some value in communicating his ideas to his contemporaries. In V.8 we may also note the prominence of Platonic myth. There is the vivid description from *Phaedrus* of the ascent of the soul to the intelligible world, which permeates the treatise, and the important idea of the divine model and the demiurge from *Timaeus.* Not only is the model a key Platonic equivalent of Plotinus' intelligible world and of the "supercelestial place" of *Phaedrus,* but also the occasion for Plotinus to "correct" the possible impression of the demiurge of *Timaeus* as an anthropomorphic figure engaged in the human cognitive activity of discursive reason, which he feels has led the Gnostics amongst others to distort the real nature of divine thought. Although he interprets both the Hesiodic myth and Platonic myths in the precise terms of his own metaphysics it is hard to avoid the impression, even in the case of the Hesiodic myth, that he has dwelt on the details not merely to embellish his presentation but also to impress more forcefully on his audience the very special and supra-rational nature of our contact with the intelligible world, which we cannot fully express in normal language. Myth, as he proclaims in his treatise *On Love* (III.5.9), has a very special role in the communication of metaphysical ideas.

We now turn to V.8 itself. The title (which, like all the titles of Plotinus' treatises, is a Porphyrian addition), and especially the first two chapters of the treatise, invite comparison with his earlier treatise *On Beauty* (I.6). Indeed these opening chapters both endorse and supplement the earlier discussion. But their context and purpose is profoundly different. I.6 is concerned with how the individual soul can return to its origins and its original beauty through the rediscovery of the successively higher levels of beauty it may be trained to encounter and recognize. The emphasis of the present treatise lies rather on the universal and cosmic dimension of beauty. Of course it is, as are most treatises of Plotinus, concerned with the individual soul—witness for example the similarity of ideas with I.6 when he suggests (V.8.9, 11–12) that we must hone the beauty in ourselves as a prerequisite for finding the beauty of others or of the intelligible universe, as well as the undoubtedly very personal and almost mystical experience of his vision of an intelligible world of interpenetrating Forms (V.8.4, 10f.). Even the opening question of the treatise: "*how* could anyone behold the beauty of intellect and of that world?" seems to point to an epistemological rather than ontological enquiry. The former will, in fact, follow in the subsequent treatise (V.5). The search for the nature of Intellect and our means of attaining it cannot easily be separated. Indeed the striking thought-experiment in Chapter 9 of V.8 demonstrates this clearly. For here in encouraging us to visualize the universe as a sphere and, by removing from our minds the notion of mass, to arrive at a concept, or rather a vision, of an intelligible universe, Plotinus is at the same time advocating the means to such vision and presenting us with the nature of that vision. As is explained below, the structure of the treatise oscillates between descriptions of the nature of intelligible beauty and the modes of cognition involved in our apprehension of it. In a sense neither is the exclusive theme, but rather the identity of the unity in plurality of the intelligible world with the highest level of our own selves, the union of universal Intellect and individual intellect. The stress is on the cosmos, that is, the intelligible cosmos with which we are one. It is, perhaps, significant in this context that when he asks us to look to and purify our own intellect he immediately invokes the intellects of the gods (3, 17f.) as models. The notion of contemplation implied here follows the tradition of astral contemplation in which it is our observation of the cosmos around us as presented by the heavenly bodies that will aid the mind to grasp the universal order which they embody, a contemplation that focuses on the cosmic totality in which man finds himself. For Plotinus this then leads the mind to encounter the gods who represent the intelligible world itself.

The notion of intelligible beauty itself requires some explanation, for it is not immediately obvious why "the *beauty* of intellect" should merit such consideration. Even though Plotinus begins his analysis from the level of physical beauty and could well have found in it the stimulus and premises to argue for the existence of beauty in the intelligible world, he will also have accepted the beauty of intellect and the intelligible world as self-evident, given the prominence of beauty as a feature of true reality in Plato. Particularly relevant in V.8 is Plato's description of the world of transcendent reality described in the central "myth" of *Phaedrus* (247f.). At 250b5–6 it is linked with beauty and our ultimate happiness: "Beauty was ours to see in all its brightness in those days when, with that happy company [of the gods], we beheld with our eyes that blessed vision." It is the same passage that Plotinus has in mind in III.8.11 and which acts as the immediate prompt to take up the subject of intellect's beauty at the beginning of V.8. Plotinus' developed metaphysical view that true being (i.e., intelligible being) is identical with beauty is a conclusion reached from a consideration of the consistency and inner structure of the nature of intelligible reality itself in the context of his interpretation of Plato. This insight is then woven into his account of the relationship of this world to its transcendent source. That the beauty of this world can then be used by the individual as a means to attain the vision of Beauty itself is the practical application of the theory.

The question with which V.8 begins, how can we see the beauty of Intellect, appears not to have been satisfactorily answered when Plotinus ends the treatise by wondering whether he has succeeded in "leading us to a clear understanding of the 'intelligible place'" or whether more is needed. The following section (V.5) looks at the intelligible world from an epistemological viewpoint, clearly indicating that this further topic was essential to complete the response to his initial enquiry. But despite Plotinus' evident insistence on continuing his enquiry, or rather going "by yet another route," the contents of V.8 do possess an integrity and completeness of their own. The conclusion that is reached is complemented rather than superseded or adjusted by V.5. It is in this sense that the study of V.8 as a single treatise is justified. It possesses, too, a clear, though complex, line of progress from its initial question to its grandiose concluding chapters with their mythical coloring.

He begins with the argument that physical beauty must come from something outside and above the matter in which it is expressed. In the case of artistic beauty (e.g., a statue) one can point to the form in the artist's mind, in that of natural beauty (e.g., a stone) to the form, which provides beauty to the underlying matter. These forms, which are higher than the immanent form they bring to matter, are more beautiful than their instantiation in the physical world.

Chapter two concludes with the call to look beyond the mere physical manifestations of beauty to the form within an object, and then yet further, away from all externals, to beauty that has no physical manifestation, for example, the goodness within someone who might even have an ugly appearance. But to attain this you must prepare yourself (make yourself beautiful).

This preparation leads us (Chapter 3) beyond discursive reason to encounter the intelligible world, the source of beauty, through the direct vision of our intellect. What this sort of cognition involves and how we can attain it provides the subject matter of the next chapters. In Chapters 4 and 5 the intelligible world is presented in terms of its *being*, in Chapter 7 as cause of *order* in the universe but itself transcending that order, while Chapter 8 returns to the theme of *beauty* to look at the intelligible world as exemplifying beauty. In this way we are brought back to the evaluation of this universe as good and beautiful (*kalon*) and to the challenge set out at the very beginning of the treatise: to explain as far as we can "how anyone could behold the beauty of intellect and of that world."

Within each of these sections our own access to the intelligible model is examined: firstly, in the context of wisdom, being and order (Chapter 6) and, then, in the context of beauty (Chapter 9). In both cases the distinction is drawn between discursive and intellectual modes of cognition. Chapters 10 to 13 expand the discussion of our mode of cognition in the context of beauty, while the main stress always falls on the goodness and beauty of the universe itself. These chapters both commence and end with myth, significantly beginning with a return to the Platonic *Phaedrus* myth (Chapters 4 and 10) of the vision of the intelligible world and concluding with the Hesiodic myth in 12 and 13, illustrating the main structural principles of Plotinus' universe, the One, Intellect, and Soul. Chapter 11 concentrates on the "how" of our vision of the intelligible world, whilst the final chapters concentrate on the nature of that world in itself and the implications for the physical universe.

Plato and Plotinus on Art as Imitation

Although Plotinus never proposes a theory of art in itself and the discussions of art in I.6 and V.8 are incidental to the main purpose of those treatises, it is nevertheless possible to abstract from them some important elements of artistic theory. And these seem directly to contradict the remarks of Plato in *Republic* X. 596a–599a, where the artist (whether painter or poet) is said to imitate reality (that is the transcendent Form) at "three removes" (597e): the carpenter "imitates" the Form of bed by looking at the Form, whereas the painter does not look at the Form, but only at its derivative (598a), the bed made by the carpenter. In V.8 Plotinus too stresses the nature of art as imitative, not however, of any physical object, as in Plato's *Republic,* but of the ideal form. In fact he further enhances the value of artistic imitation by placing his analysis of it before and introductory to his explanation of natural imitation. In this context he notes that the artist can even improve on nature (V.8.1, 36–37). In these respects Plotinus' view of art does not follow Plato's analysis of art as presented in *Republic* X, but echoes rather the metaphysics of the *Symposium*, where beauty is traced back to its transcendent cause, and the status of art (poetry) in the *Phaedrus*, where it is an expression of divine inspiration. Presumably Plotinus would not see a contradiction here, but would suppose that in the *Republic* Plato is considering a different context (politics or education) and, perhaps also, a different kind of art, one on a lower level. Hence possibly his refusal to have his portrait painted (Porphyry, *Life of Plotinus* 1), since this really would be at a third remove, an imitation of a particular physical reality. The sort of art that Plotinus perhaps has in mind in V.8 is the kind of idealistic sculpture represented by Pheidias' statue of Zeus at Olympia, mentioned at the end of the first chapter. The ground seems already to have been prepared for such an "idealizing" trend in interpreting Plato. It appears already in Cicero (*Orator* 2.8–3.9) and in Seneca (*Letter* 65.8); in the latter as a combination of Stoic, Platonic, and Aristotelian doctrines that probably goes back to Antiochus, a Stoicizing Platonist of the first century BCE. An interesting similarity of approach may also be found in the discussion by Dio of Prusa, an orator and cynic of the second century CE, of Pheidias' Zeus in his *Olympian Oration* (*Oration* 12), where he makes Pheidias defend his representation of the god in human form and show that it does not diminish his real stature. All of this suggests that Plotinus was not out of touch with contemporary theories of art and, far from criticizing Plato, would have thought that he was correctly interpreting Plato's "real intent" against possible misinterpretation.

Another reason, too, for Plotinus' positive evaluation of artistic beauty may lie in his exploration of the way in which we make the ascent to the intelligible world. It is significant that Plotinus begins the treatise V.8 with an analysis of artistic rather than natural beauty. This stress on artistic beauty and its explanation in terms of form and apprehension of form is fuelled by his own optimistic view of the ability of man to reach the level of Intellect and its beauty, particularly since for him the individual intellect then becomes one with the universal Intellect. The idea that the artist has within him an idea of beauty that derives directly from the intelligible world in fact coincides with his theory that each one of us has access to Intellect through his own intellect. And it is the exploitation of this theme that forms the central dynamic of the treatise, with its stress on our ability to "see" and be one with the intelligible world and its beauty.

Note on the Greek Text

LINE NUMBERS IN THE TRANSLATION are approximate and do not always match the original Greek text. Since the commentary follows the sequence of the English translation, there may sometimes be a slight discrepancy in the ordering.

The Greek text adopted is that of the Oxford edition, that is, the *editio minor* (for comparison between readings in HS_1 and HS_2 see vol. 3, xiii–xiv). Deviations from the text are noted in the commentary.

Each *Ennead* is referred to by Roman numerals, followed by the number of the treatise, the chapter of the treatise, and, finally, separated by a comma, the line number or numbers, for example, VI.8.8, 24–27, that is, *Ennead* VI, treatise number 8, Chapter 8, lines 24–27.

It is customary to add the chronological number given by Porphyry in his *Life of Plotinus* (*Vita Plotini*), so that, for example, VI.8 is designated VI.8 [39], that is, *Ennead* VI.8 is 39th in the chronological order. So we adopt the convention as follows: either VI.8.8, 1–5 (where the chronological number is not given) or VI.8 [39] 8, 1–5 (where it is given).

In this series the chronological number is given only in the Introduction and in other places where it may be of significance for understanding the chronological presentation of Plotinus' philosophical stance. The following chart indicates the chronological order.

Chronological Order of the *Enneads*

Enn.		*Enn.*		*Enn.*		*Enn.*		*Enn.*		*Enn.*	
I.1	**53**	II.1	**40**	III.1	**3**	IV.1	**21**	V.1	**10**	VI.1	**42**
I.2	**19**	II.2	**14**	III.2	**47**	IV.2	**4**	V.2	**11**	VI.2	**43**
I.3	**20**	II.3	**52**	III.3	**48**	IV.3	**27**	V.3	**49**	VI.3	**44**
I.4	**46**	II.4	**12**	III.4	**15**	IV.4	**28**	V.4	**7**	VI.4	**22**
I.5	**36**	II.5	**25**	III.5	**50**	IV.5	**29**	V.5	**32**	VI.5	**23**
I.6	**1**	II.6	**17**	III.6	**26**	IV.6	**41**	V.6	**24**	VI.6	**34**
I.7	**54**	II.7	**37**	III.7	**45**	IV.7	**2**	V.7	**18**	VI.7	**38**
I.8	**51**	II.8	**35**	III.8	**30**	IV.8	**6**	V.8	**31**	VI.8	**39**
I.9	**16**	II.9	**33**	III.9	**13**	IV.9	**8**	V.9	**5**	VI.9	**9**

	Enn.		*Enn.*		*Enn.*		*Enn.*		*Enn.*		*Enn.*
1	I.6	**10**	V.1	**19**	I.2	**28**	IV.4	**37**	II.7	**46**	I.4
2	IV.7	**11**	V.2	**20**	I.3	**29**	IV.5	**38**	VI.7	**47**	III.2
3	III.1	**12**	II.4	**21**	IV.1	**30**	III.8	**39**	VI.8	**48**	III.3
4	IV.2	**13**	III.9	**22**	VI.4	**31**	V.8	**40**	II.1	**49**	V.3
5	V.9	**14**	II.2	**23**	VI.5	**32**	V.5	**41**	IV.6	**50**	III.5
6	IV.8	**15**	III.4	**24**	V.6	**33**	II.9	**42**	VI.1	**51**	I.8
7	V.4	**16**	I.9	**25**	II.5	**34**	VI.6	**43**	VI.2	**52**	II.3
8	IV.9	**17**	II.6	**26**	III.6	**35**	II.8	**44**	VI.3	**53**	I.1
9	VI.9	**18**	V.7	**27**	IV.3	**36**	I.5	**45**	III.7	**54**	I.7

Synopsis

Chapter 1

1–6 How may we see intelligible beauty?

6–21 We must start with physical beauty and by distinguishing natural and artistic beauty (a stone and sculptured stone). A portrait bust is beautiful because of the form imposed on it which was in the artist through his share in art. But the beauty in the bust is inferior to the beauty that remains in art.

21–27 Form enters matter as immanent form, while the transcendent form remains. Stone submits to form but the transcendent form is more beautiful than the immanent form which becomes progressively weaker as it enters into matter.

27–32 Everything becomes weaker as it descends. The higher the maker the stronger it is. An effect is not achieved by its absence but by a cause which produces the effect as its image.

32–34 Do not despise art because it imitates nature since nature too imitates [transcendent form].

34–40 Art goes back to the original form (which is also the source for nature) and even adds what is missing [the idealized statue?].

Chapter 2

1–16 Beauty in nature: its beauty is not found primarily in the external matter but in the form within, which comes from the maker.

17–21 But if the external mass is beautiful as mass, the form cannot be the cause of its beauty.

21–28 But mass cannot be the cause of beauty since the same sort of beauty is found in things of different size. Physical beauty is perceived as immanent form along with externally expressed attributes such as size taken in through the eyes, small as they are.

28–38 If the maker were ugly it could not produce what is beautiful. Nature is prior in beauty to the things it makes but we are often satisfied with the external and remain unaware of the cause of beauty lying invisibly within things.

38–41 An ugly face may even hide an internal moral beauty.

41–46 But if you fail to recognize this beauty you will not discover what is beautiful within yourself.

Chapter 3

1–10 This internal logos may be found at different levels: in nature, the soul, the soul of the good man; its cause is intellect.

11–19 We can form an idea of this primal beauty of intellect by appealing to our own intellect or to the intellect of the gods, who are beautiful.

19–30 The gods are beautiful not because of their bodies but their intellects, which are always active in contemplation of Intellect itself.

30–36 The incorporeal gods at the level of Intellect are one with it. Everything is there as one, the entire earth including animals and men.

Chapter 4

1–11 In the intelligible world all is one and everything is in everything else.

11–27 There movement is compatible with rest. There is no distinction between what a thing is and its substrate; each part is at the same time the whole.

27–36 The inexhaustible contemplation of the intelligible world is not accompanied by weariness or surfeit.

36–44 It is both primary wisdom and being.

44–48 Its great power is seen in it being cause of all. It has produced all things within itself, and is identical with them. Its wisdom is identical with its being.

48–56 But we fail to grasp it because we think in terms of discursive reason. But for Plato its substrate is identical with what it is. It is our duty as philosophers to explore what this wisdom means.

Chapter 5

1–9 Wisdom is the source of all creation whether natural or artistic. In fact the artist goes back to nature in the form of his own intellect, which transcends discursive abstractions.

9–25 True wisdom and true being are identical at the level of intellect. The gods are not looking at axioms but what really exists, the Ideas.

Chapter 6

1–9 Wisdom, like the symbols in Egyptian temples, is beyond letters, words and discursive reasoning.

10–19 An immanent wisdom, the image of transcendent wisdom, is accessible to discursive reasoning and points to the existence of transcendent wisdom.

Chapter 7

1–11 The All provides an example of this. Although it displays planning and order, its creator (transcendent wisdom) did not plan and order like a craftsman.

12–17 This universe is a direct and immediate product of the intelligible archetype in which everything is together.

17–25 It is composed of layers of forms, the effortless product of transcendent form.

26–28 If this world is an All its maker is an All. Even if it has internal restrictions, its totality as an All is not restricted.

28–35 By becoming "man" we have lost our share in the activity of making, but can regain it by rising to the divine level.

36–47 Assigning reasons for the arrangement of the universe does not entail that it was planned through reasoning. Its production is prior to reasoning.

Chapter 8

1–5 The intelligible model is beautiful in the primary sense that it is entirely beautiful.

5–7 The One is beyond beauty but Intellect delights in contemplating beauty as its object.

7–20 So Plato (*Timaeus* 37c–d1) in describing the demiurge as delighting in the universe implies that he is contemplating the model of which it is the image.

21–23 The only valid criticism of the beauty of this world is that it does not possess the primary beauty of the intelligible world.

Chapter 9

1–26 We must imagine a picture of our physical universe, then, placing beside it another universe devoid of the restrictions of space and matter, and conceive of its plurality in unity.

26–35 This universe as an image is also great, but the powers operating in it conflict with each other to effect generation and destruction.

35–42 In the intelligible world being and beauty are one.

42–47 But in this world beauty is brought in from outside.

Chapter 10

1–22 Zeus (Plato *Phaedrus* 246e4–6) leads the other gods and souls in contemplation of Beauty which each sees in a different way, sometimes, in contemplation, even present in its entirety.

22–29 The final vision is of beauty illuminating the whole of being, which illuminates us too so that we become beautiful.

29–43 And just as in the intelligible, beauty is identical with being, so we too must no longer see ourselves as beautiful but as being beauty.

Chapter 11

1–19 How we may make the step from seeing an image of ourselves as beautiful to coming into union with the Beautiful. The former state is a preparation for entering the inner self.

19–40 When we have reached this stage we are no longer aware of the state we are in, just as a healthy man remains unaware of his health because it is his natural state. So, too, real knowledge is present silently and imperceptibly.

Chapter 12

1–13 An intimation of the intelligible world is communicated to us through Zeus, its final manifestation, who as the image of that world reflects its beauty as our universe.

13–20 The intelligible world must always produce an image and one that is beautiful, and has life and eternity.

20–26 It is wrong to claim that this universe is not eternal and that it was planned to exist for a particular time. But the limitations of human discourse compel us to use the vocabulary of conscious planning and creation.

Chapter 13

1–11 Kronos, representing the Intelligible World, looks above to Ouranos (the One) and hands over control of the physical universe to his son Zeus (Soul) below him.

11–20 Ouranos is beyond beauty, Kronos (Intellect) is primary beauty, Zeus (Soul) is less beautiful as having only a trace of beauty; Aphrodite (the World soul) is also beautiful because of her relationship to the Intelligible World.

20–22 We too are beautiful when we return to our true self and know ourselves.

22–24 Perhaps we need to explain in a different way how we reach the intelligible world.

Translation of Plotinus
Ennead *V.8 [31]*

On Intelligible Beauty

1. Since we affirm that the man who has acquired the vision of the intelligible world and has intellectually perceived the beauty of true intellect can also conceive of its father and what transcends it, let us attempt to see and express to ourselves, | insofar as it is possible to express such matters, how anyone could behold the beauty of intellect and of that world.

Well now, let us imagine two solid stones lying beside each other, one without regular shape and untouched by art, the other already mastered by art to form a statue of a god, | one of the Graces, or a Muse, for example, or even of a man, not any man but one whom art has created incorporating all the beautiful elements available to it. The one which has become beautiful in form through art would appear beautiful not from its being a stone—for the other one would then be equally beautiful—but from the form which art has imposed on it. | This form then is not something which the matter possessed, but it was in the one who thought it even before it came into the stone. And it was in the craftsman not because he possessed eyes and hands but because he had a share in art; and this beauty was, therefore, in art in a much more superior manner, for the beauty in art did not come into the stone, | but it remains [in its source] while another comes from it, inferior to it.

And not even this remained pure in the stone nor as it wanted to be, but only so far as the stone yielded to art. But if art makes a thing to be like what it itself is and possesses, that is, makes it beautiful in accordance with the rational principle of the thing it is making, it is itself beautiful to a greater degree and more authentically [than what it makes], as it possesses the beauty which belongs to art, a beauty which is greater and more beautiful | than the beauty present in the external object. For the more the latter becomes extended by proceeding into matter, the weaker it is compared with the beauty that remains in unity. For everything that is extended draws apart from itself: in the case of strength, it loses strength, in the case of heat, it becomes less hot, in that of power in general, less powerful, and of beauty, | less beautiful. And that which is the primary maker must in every case be more powerful than what is made. For it is not lack of music that makes a man musical, but music, and the music that is in the sensible world is made by the music prior to this world.

And if anyone belittles the arts because they make by imitating nature, we must firstly say that natural things too imitate other things. One must also realize that the arts do not simply imitate what can be seen but | go back to the rational principles from which nature derives. And one must further understand that they do much on their own initiative and even add something to anything that is deficient, because they possess beauty, since Pheidias too did not make his Zeus by looking at anything visible to the eyes but by grasping what | Zeus would be like if he had cared to manifest himself to our eyes.

2. But let us put aside the arts and look at what they are said to be imitations of, the things that are and are said to be natural beauties, all rational and irrational creatures and particularly those of them that are successful when what has shaped and created them | has mastered the matter and provided it with the form that it intended. What then is beauty in these? For it certainly isn't the blood and the menstrual fluid. But the beauty of natural things is also not their color, which is always changing, nor their external shape. It is either nothing or something without shape or something simple like that which circumscribes. What then caused | the beauty of Helen, for whom men

fought, to shine forth, or that of women who are like Aphrodite in beauty? And whence too in fact the beauty of Aphrodite herself or in general of any handsome man or god from amongst those who can enter into our sight, or even of those who cannot but possess in themselves a beauty which can be seen?

Surely in each case it is form, which is the cause, that comes from the maker | to the thing that comes into being, just as in the case of the arts form was said to come from the arts upon artistic creations.

What does this mean? Are the things made and the rational principle imposed on matter beautiful, but the rational principle that is not in matter but in the maker, the very primary and immaterial principle, is not to be counted as beauty?

But if mass is beautiful | insofar as it is mass, it follows that rational principle which is the maker, because it is not mass, is not beautiful.

But if, when the same form is in something small and something large, it stimulates and affects the soul of the person who sees it in equal measure by its power, the beauty of the object must not be assigned to the magnitude of its mass. Further evidence of this is the fact that | while something is outside us we do not yet perceive it, but it affects us when it comes within. But it enters through the eyes as form alone; for if it were more than form how could it enter through something as small as the eye? But the size too is brought in with it, not large in mass, but becoming large in form.

Moreover the maker must be either ugly, indifferent or beautiful. If it was ugly | it could not make its opposite; if it was indifferent why would it rather make something beautiful than something ugly? But in fact nature, which makes things which are so beautiful, is far prior to them in beauty while we, because we are not accustomed to see anything of the things within and do not know them, pursue what is external without realizing that it is what is within that moves us. It is just as if someone | were to look at and pursue an image of himself without knowing its origin. But the beauty in learning, in moral behavior and in souls demonstrates that what is pursued is something else and beauty is not found in magnitude. And it really is a greater beauty than that [external beauty] when you see moral goodness in someone and rejoice in it, not | looking at his face, for this could be ugly, but pursue his inner beauty, leaving aside all external form. But if it does not yet move you to say that such a one is beautiful you will not, when looking within into yourself, rejoice in its beauty. If you are in this state you will search in vain for the beauty within you, for you will be searching with what is ugly and not pure. | It is for this reason that discussions about such matters are not directed at all men. But if you have seen yourself as beautiful, remember them.

3. There is, then, in nature a rational principle, which is the archetype of the beauty found in body, and the principle in the soul is more beautiful than the one in nature; and the one in nature is derived from it. Clearest of all is the rational principle in the soul of the good man, and it is even prior in beauty because it has brought order | to the soul and, by providing it with light from a greater light, which is beauty in a primary way, it is itself responsible, by being present in the soul, for making the soul conclude what sort of thing is the principle that is prior to it and which has not actually come to be [in the soul] nor in anything else, but is in itself. For this reason it is not even a rational principle but the maker of the primary rational principle which is the beauty present in the soul, that acts as matter for it; and this is intellect |, the intellect that operates always and not intermittently, because it is not brought in to itself from outside.

What image could we take for it? For every image is drawn from something inferior. But then the image must come from intellect, in such a way that we do not conceive it by means of an image but like taking a portion of gold as an indicator of an entire gold piece; and if the gold that has been taken is not pure, we must purify it by deed | and word to show that this piece in its entirety is not gold but only the gold content in the piece. In the same way in this case too we may conceive from our intellect, once it has been purified, and from the gods, if you wish, what sort of thing their intellect is. For all the gods are august and beautiful, and their "beauty" is "immense."[3]

But what is it | that makes them like this?

Surely it is intellect, and it is because intellect is more active in them that it is visible. For their beauty is not visible because their bodies are beautiful; for even for those who have bodies it is not this fact that makes them gods. But they too are gods in virtue of their intellect. And they are in fact beautiful in so far as they are gods; for they are not mentally active at one moment and not at the next, | but are always mentally active in an intellection that is unaffected, stable and pure, and they know everything and are acquainted not with human but with their own divine concerns and with whatever Intellect sees.

The gods in the heavens are always contemplating, as it were from a distance, the things in that other heaven by raising | their heads on high—for they have the time for this—while those that are in that heaven whose sojourn is on and in it [contemplate] while dwelling in the whole of that higher heaven. For everything there is heaven, and the earth is heaven as well as the sea and living creatures and plants and men; everything belonging to that higher heaven is heavenly. And the gods who are in it do not despise men | or any of the other things there, because

3 Plato *Republic* 509a6 of the idea of the Good, and *Symposium* 218e1 of the inner beauty of Socrates.

they belong there. Rather they journey the length and breadth of that land and region, though always at rest.

4. For the "easy life" is found there and truth is their mother, nurse, being, and nourishment. And they see everything: not the things to which "becoming is added"[4] but those that have being. And they see themselves in others; for everything there is transparent and nothing is | dark or resistant, but every god is transparent to every other god to the innermost core and in every detail; for light is transparent to light and each has everything in himself and also sees everything in another, so that everything is everywhere, everything is everything, each is everything and the radiance is unbounded. For each of the things there is great since the small, too, is great; and | the sun there is all the stars and each star is the sun and all the stars. There stands out in each something different, but all, too, are clearly manifest. Movement too is pure, for what causes motion does not disturb movement as it proceeds because it is not different from it. And rest is not disturbed because it is not mixed with what is not stable. And the beautiful is beautiful because it is not | in what is not beautiful. Each walks not as it were on alien ground but each one's place is identical with its very self. And when it ascends, as it were, on high, the place it came

4 Plato *Phaedrus* 247d7.

from accompanies it; and it is not one thing and its place another, for its substrate is intellect and it is itself intellect. It is as if one were to think that in this our heaven |, which is visible and is full of light, the light from it was born as the stars. But in this heaven one part would then come from another part and each would be only a part, whereas there each part always comes from a whole, whilst at the same time remaining as both part and whole. It appears in fact as a part, but on closer inspection is seen to be a whole, | supposing that one was as keen-eyed as Lynceus; he was said to see even the things inside the earth in a myth that allegorically suggests the [sort of] eyes present in the transcendent world.

The vision of what is there brings no weariness nor surfeit that leads the beholder to seek for rest, because there was no emptying that would lead them to be sated when they had been filled and reached their goal. | Nor is one thing different from another in such a way that the characteristics of one would not be pleasing to another of those in it [i.e., the intelligible world]. The things there are never wearied. And not being filled there entails the absence of that fullness that causes contempt for what has caused the filling; for when it sees it goes on seeing more and more, and in seeing itself and the objects of its vision as unbounded it is going along with its own nature. | Moreover, life never brings weariness to anyone when it is pure; then why would that which lives the best life become weary?

This life is wisdom, but a wisdom that is not supplied by reasoning, because it is always entire and not deficient in anything so that it needs to search. But it is the primary wisdom and not derived from another. And being is itself wisdom, but not in the sense of being first itself and then wise. | For this reason there is no greater wisdom than this. And Knowledge itself is there enthroned beside Intellect by being manifest together, just as they say allegorically that Justice is beside Zeus. For all such things there are like statues seen on their own terms so that "they are a vision for most blessed viewers."[5]

Then one would see | the magnitude of this wisdom and its power, because of the fact that it possesses and has made along with itself all that is; and everything followed it, and it is itself the things that are which came into being along with it, and both are one, and being is identical with the wisdom that is there. But we have not reached an understanding of it because we have come to think that knowledge consists of abstract theorems and the combining | of propositions. But anyone who is uncertain about the latter should put aside the discussion of them for the moment. But with regard to knowledge there, Plato actually perceived it when he said that it "is

5 Plato *Phaedo* 111a3 of the real earth as opposed to the murky hollows in which we live.

not different from that in which it is,”[6] but how it is so he left to us to seek and discover, if we are | worthy of the name of philosopher.

So then it is perhaps better to start from this point:

5. In fact all things that come into being, whether artificial or natural, are made by some kind of wisdom. And wisdom everywhere guides making. But if someone really does make in accordance with wisdom itself, we must grant that the arts are like this. But the craftsman in turn | goes back to the wisdom of nature, by which he has himself come into being, a wisdom which is no longer composed of abstract theorems, but is whole as some one thing, not put together from many to make one but rather capable of being resolved into a plurality from one. Then if anyone makes this the primary wisdom, that will be satisfactory; for it would not be wisdom derived from something else or in something else.

But if they say the wisdom [employed by the artist] is | the reason principle in nature and its source is nature, we will ask where does nature have it from and whether it has derived it from another. If it has it from itself, we will stop there. But if they go on to intellect, we must then look at whether intellect has generated wisdom. And if they say it has, we must ask from where. If it is from itself,

6 Plato *Phaedrus* 247d7–e1.

that is impossible unless it is itself intellect. | Then true wisdom is being and true being is wisdom. And being has its value from wisdom and, because it is from wisdom, it is true being as well. For this reason too, beings which do not possess wisdom, by virtue of the fact that they are brought into existence through some wisdom, do possess being, but, because they do not have wisdom in themselves, are not beings in the true sense. | And so one should not suppose that the gods, and those who are exceedingly happy there, are looking at axioms there, but each of the things we are speaking about are beautiful images there like those that someone imagined were in the soul of a wise man, but not images that are drawn, but ones that really exist. It is for this reason that the ancients, too, said that the Ideas are realities and substances.

6. I think that the Egyptian wise men too, whether they grasp this by precise or by innate knowledge, when they want to indicate something in a wise manner, do not make use of inscribed letters which systematically lead to words and propositions and imitate sounds and | the utterance of axioms, but, by engraving images and inscribing in their temples a single image for each particular thing, make clear the non-discursiveness of wisdom there, and so indicate that each image is a form of knowledge, wisdom, substrate and all together at once, and not discursive thought or deliberation.

But | from wisdom itself which is all together, at a later stage, a secondary image is deployed in something else, one which expresses itself discursively and lays open the causes by which it is what it is, so as to excite admiration since what has come to be is so beautiful. Anyone who knows this will say how amazing it is how this [immanent] wisdom which does not itself contain the causes of being, provides them | to the things that are made in accordance with it. For this reason, then, that which is so beautiful and could scarcely or not at all be revealed by research to be necessarily like this, [must,] if one were to discover it, exist as it is before research and reasoning. For example—for let us take what I mean in the case of one large example, which will also be applicable to all the rest—

7. this All: since we agree that its existence and its being the way it is derives from something else, are we then to suppose that its maker went through the process of thinking to himself of earth and that earth had to take its place in the middle [of the universe] and next water and that this had to rest upon earth, and the others | in order right up to the heavens, and after this all the animals and in their case the forms of each one such as they are now, as well as their inner organs and external parts, and that when he had them all appropriately arranged in his mind he had then to set to work? But conceiving of things in this way is impossible, for where would it have come from to

one who had never seen such things? | Nor is it possible by taking such things from another to make them, as do craftsmen who use their hands and tools; for hands and feet come later.

Then it remains that everything is in another and that, since nothing exists in-between because of the close neighborhood of all things to each other in real being, an appearance and | image of the intelligible is all at once, as it were, made manifest, whether from real being itself or from soul acting as facilitator—this makes no difference in the present discussion—or from a particular soul. But everything in this world, then, comes from there and is in a more beautiful state there. For what is here is mixed but those there are not. This world, then, is held together by forms from beginning to end: matter, | first of all, by the forms of the elements, then other forms on these forms, then again further forms on these. This is also the reason why it is difficult to discover matter, which is hidden beneath these many forms. And since matter too is a sort of ultimate form, this world is entirely form and consisting of forms, for its model was form. And it was made without noise since what made it was entirely | being and form. For this reason its creation was also without toil.

And it is the creation of what is an All so that [its maker] must be an All. Moreover there was nothing to hinder its creating and even now it dominates even though one thing hinders another, but nothing is a hindrance to it; for it remains as an All.

And I think that we, too, if we were archetypes and being and forms all at once | and the form which makes here were our being, our creative activity would dominate without effort. Man, however, produces a form other than himself, having become what he now is; for by now becoming man he has separated himself from being the All. But if he ceases to be man, as Plato says, "he walks on high and | orders the whole cosmos";[7] for when he comes to belong to the whole he makes the whole.

But to return to the original purpose of our discussion; you are able to give a reason for the earth's being in the middle [of the universe] and why it is spherical and why the ecliptic is as it is, but it was not planned there because it had to be the way it is, but rather because it is as it is there, it follows that things here too | are beautifully arranged. It is as if the conclusion was there before the syllogism which contained the cause, and was not derived from the premises. For this universe did not come about as a result of a logical sequence and from consideration, but is prior to logical sequence and consideration. For all of these are later, along with reasoning, demonstration and conviction. For since there is a principle [the intelligible world], all of these follow from it in the way they

7 Plato *Phaedrus* 246c1–2.

are. | And for this reason it is well said that one should not search for the causes of a principle, and of a principle of this kind, that is, perfect, and which is identical with its end. And any principle that is also an end is everything together and lacking in nothing.

8. Who then would not call beautiful that which is beautiful in the primary sense, and whole and whole throughout, in the sense that none of its parts fails by a deficiency in beauty? For one would not call primarily beautiful what is not itself beautiful as a whole, but has a part of beauty or none of it at all. Otherwise if that is not beautiful, what else is? | For that which is prior to it has no desire to be beautiful. For that which is the first to present itself for contemplation by being form and object of vision for Intellect is the thing that is a delight to behold. And it is for this reason that Plato,[8] wanting to indicate this with reference to something more familiar to ourselves, makes the demiurge bestow his approval on the completed world, meaning to show | through this how delightful is the beauty of the model and the Idea. For whenever someone admires anything modeled on something else, he directs his admiration to that on which it has been modeled.

And if a person is unaware of what is happening to him, that is nothing to be surprised about, since lovers

8 Plato *Timaeus* 37c7–d1.

too and people in general who admire beauty in this world are unaware that they do so because of intelligible beauty. For that | is the cause.

That he applies the phrase "was delighted" to the model he deliberately makes clear in the following words he uses when he says: "he was both delighted and wanted to make it still more like the model itself"; in this way showing what the beauty of the model is | by saying that what has become beautiful has become so because of the model since it is its image.

And if, then, the intelligible were not exceedingly beautiful "with an unbounded beauty," what would be more beautiful than this universe that we can see? And so those who find fault with this world are wrong, except in so far as it is not the intelligible world.

9. Then let us grasp this world by means of discursive reason, with each of its parts remaining what it is without confusion, brought into one whole "all together," as far as is possible, so that when any one part appears, for example the sphere which is outside the world, there immediately accompanies it a representation | of the sun as well, together with the other stars; and earth, sea and all living creatures are seen, just as everything could in fact also be seen in a transparent sphere. Let there be then in your soul a luminous representation of a sphere, containing in it everything whether moving or still, in fact definitely

both | what is moving and what is still. And while you keep hold of this representation take another beside you [into your self], but with the mass removed. And remove both the places and the image of matter in yourself; and do not be tempted to take another sphere that is smaller than it in mass, but call on the god who made the sphere whose image you have and pray for him to come. | May he come, bringing his own world with all the gods which are within it, he who is one and all; and each of them is all coming together in one; they are different in powers, but all are one by that single multiple power. Rather, the one is all; for he is not himself deficient by the fact that all those gods come into existence. They are all together and each is separate as well in a non-spatial fixity | since none has any perceptible shape—if it did one would be here and another there, and each would not be the whole in itself; nor does any have parts different from other parts or from itself [as a whole]; nor is each like a power that has been cut up and is co-extensive with the enumerated parts, but each one | is the entire power, extending to infinity and powerful to infinity. And that god is so great that even his parts are infinite; for where can you name anything that he has not already reached?

This universe, then, is also great and all the powers together within it, but it would be greater, | and how much more so one could not say, if the petty power of body were not present in it. And yet one could still claim that the powers of fire and other bodies were great; but it is only because of our inexperience of true power that they appear to burn, destroy, exercise pressure and work toward the generation of living creatures. | But these things destroy because they themselves are subject to destruction and help to generate because they are also themselves generated. But the power of the intelligible world possesses only its existence and its being beautiful. For where would its beauty be if it were deprived of its existence? And where would its being be if it were bereft of being beautiful? For if it were deficient in beauty it would also be deficient | in being. It is for this reason, too, that existence is desirable because it is identical with beauty, and beauty is lovable because it is existence. And what need is there to ask which is the cause of which when their nature is one? But the false being of this universe does require beauty brought in as an image for it even to appear to be beautiful or to exist at all. | And it exists in so far as it shares in the beauty endowed by form. And, when it has taken on beauty, the more it does so the more perfect it becomes. For its being is enhanced in proportion to its beauty.

10. For this reason "Zeus," although he is the most senior of the other gods whom he himself leads, "comes first" to the contemplation of this god while the other gods, spirits,

and souls which are able to view these things "follow."[9] | He [the Beautiful] appears to them from some invisible place and, having risen high above them, illuminated everything, filled it with his rays and dazzled those below, and they turn away unable to see him like the sun. Then some can bear it and look at him, while others are troubled the more they have separated themselves | from him.

But those who can see, when they do so, all look upon him and what belongs to him. But each does not always acquire the same vision, but one who looks intensely sees the source and nature shining forth, another is filled with the vision of moral probity [*sophrosyne*], not the kind which men experience | in themselves, when they do possess it; for this is somehow an imitation of that there. But [that beauty] over all that plays upon what you could call its entire immensity is the final thing seen by those who have already seen many clear visions, the gods both individually and all together, and souls which see everything there and are generated from everything, so that | they embrace everything themselves too from beginning to end. And they are there as much as they can naturally be there; and often even the whole of them is there whenever they are not divided.

And so Zeus sees these things, as does any of us who is a fellow-lover[10] with him; and last of all he sees the

9 Plato *Phaedrus* 246e4–6; 248a1.

10 See Plato *Phaedrus* 249e4.

beauty which remains whole over all and the beauty he partakes | is the beauty there. For it shines on all and fills those who have come to be there so that they too themselves become beautiful, like men who make the ascent to high places, where the earth has a sandy-red color, are themselves filled with that color and are made like the earth on which they have set foot. But in the intelligible world | the color that blooms on it is beauty; rather it is all color and beauty from its innermost depths. For its color is not something different from itself as though it were blooming on the surface. For those who do not see the whole note only the first impression, whereas those who are thoroughly, as it were, drunk and filled with nectar,[11] since beauty has penetrated their entire soul, | are become more than mere spectators. For there is no longer one external thing and another external thing looking at it, but one who looks keenly has what is seen within himself; and though he has it for the most part he is unaware that he has it and he looks at it as though it were external, because he looks at it as something seen and because he wants to look at it. But he must | now bring it into himself and look at it as being one and look at it as being himself, as if someone, taken over by Phoebus and possessed by a god or by a Muse, were to make the

11 Plato *Symposium* 203b5.

vision of god within himself, if he had the power to see god within his own self.

11. Any of us still unable to see himself, when he is possessed by that god and brings forth the vision to behold, brings forth himself and looks at an image of himself that has been made beautiful; but after letting go the image, however beautiful it is, and coming into unity with himself, | no longer splitting himself, he is all one together with that god silently present and is with him as far as he can and wants to be. But if he turns to being two, as long as he remains pure he is just next to him, so that he can be present to him again in that other way, if he turns back again to him. In this turning he has the following gain: | he begins by perceiving himself while he is different from the god; but as he proceeds inward he possesses everything, and leaving perception behind him through his fear of being different, he is one in the intelligible world. And if he wants to see the god as different he has only to make himself external. And while he is learning about this god he must maintain an impression of him and | in his search must "discriminate"[12] what kind of thing he is entering into. And once he has learned with confidence that he is entering into something most blessed, he must now give himself over to his inner self and instead of one

12 Plato *Republic* 516e8 used of the prisoner who returns to the cave to compete with the other prisoners in distinguishing shadows.

who sees now become an object of vision for another to contemplate, shining forth with the sort of thoughts which come from that world.

How, then, can someone be in beauty | if he does not see it?

In fact if he sees it as other than himself he is not yet in beauty; but when he becomes it he is then very much in beauty. Then if sight is of something external, sight is not what is needed, unless it is sight which is identical with its object, that is, a sort of understanding or perception of itself which takes care not to stand apart from itself by wanting to perceive too much. One should | also consider the fact that the perceptions of evils have greater impacts but bring less knowledge, because it is beaten out by the impact. For illness makes the greater impact, whereas health, which is silently present, gives the greater understanding of itself. For it cleaves to us, as being something that belongs to us and is one with us. But illness is something alien and | does not belong to us and for this reason very obvious because it seems to be altogether very different from us. And we also have no perception of what belongs to us. And because we are like this we have a particular understanding of everything belonging to ourselves when we have made our self-knowledge and ourselves one. And so in that world, when we most intensely know in an intellectual way, we seem to be ignorant, since we are waiting for the experience of perception |, which is saying that it has not seen. For it has not seen, nor ever could see such things. Perception, then, is what does not believe and the other is the one who sees. Indeed if he too were to disbelieve, he would not even believe in his own existence. For he cannot put himself outside as an object to be viewed and look at himself with his bodily eyes.

12. But we have said how a man can contemplate intellect from the point of view of his being other than it and how he can do this by himself being it. But when he does see, whether as other or as himself, what does he report? Surely that he has seen a god in labor with a beautiful child who has moreover generated everything within himself | with painless labor within. For he is pleased with what he has produced, rejoices in his children and has kept everything with him, gladly acknowledging his own and their glory. But from the rest of these children, who are beautiful, and more beautiful for remaining within, one child alone, Zeus, has appeared outside. And from him, who is the last child, | it is possible to see, from an image, as it were, of his father, how great are his father and his brothers who remained with him. But, he says, he did not come from his father in vain, for his other universe must exist, coming into being as beautiful, since it is an image of a universe that is beautiful. For it is not proper that there should not be a beautiful image of beauty and | of being.

In fact it imitates the archetype in every respect. For it has life and what belongs to being, since it is an imitation, as well as its being beauty, since it is from that higher world. And it also has its eternity, as an image. Otherwise it [the intelligible world] will sometimes have an image and sometimes not, not an image produced by art; but every natural image exists as long as the archetype | remains. For this reason they are wrong who destroy this world while the intelligible world remains, and who generate it as if its creator planned to make it at some particular time. For they do not want to understand the manner of its creation, nor do they even realize that as long as that higher shines forth, the rest can never fail, and that this world also exists as a result of the existence of that higher reality; | and it always was and will be. Unfortunately we have to employ this sort of vocabulary because of our need to express our meaning.

13. Therefore the god who is bound so as to remain the same and who has given his son the charge of this universe—for it was not in character for him to abandon his rule in the universe there and pursue a newer and later rule for himself because he had had enough of beauties—| has let this world go and established his own father in himself, and [extends] as far as him in the upward direction. And he has also established what lies in the other direction, beginning from his son, to be after him, so that

he comes to be between both by the otherness due to his being cut off from what is above and the bond which keeps him above what comes after him and which lie | below; he is thus situated between a better father and a worse son. But since his father [Ouranos/the One] was too great to be designated beauty, he [Kronos/Intellect] is the one who remains beautiful in a primary way, although soul too is beautiful. But he is more beautiful even than soul because soul has a trace of him and is beautiful in its nature because of this, but all the more beautiful | when it looks above. And so if, to speak in more familiar terms, the soul of the universe, that is Aphrodite herself, is beautiful, what is he? For if soul is beautiful from itself, what would be the greatness of that beauty there? If soul has it from another, from whom does it have the beauty that comes from outside and is yet consonant with its own being? Since we too, when | we are beautiful, are so by belonging to ourselves, and ugly when we change to another nature; and when we know ourselves we are beautiful, but ugly when we are ignorant of ourselves, beauty then is in that higher world and comes from there.

Is, then, what we have said sufficient to lead us to a clear understanding of the "intelligible place"[13] or must we go there by yet another route, as in what follows?[14]

---

13 Plato *Republic* 508c1; 517b5.

14 I.e., V.5 [32] 1, etc.

Commentary

Chapter 1

To establish the nature of the beauty of the intelligible world, he traces the cause of beauty in the physical world, beginning with the beauty of manmade objects. The ultimately Platonic notion of art as imitation is expressed positively in terms of his own interpretation of Platonic metaphysics, in which all production is seen as a product of contemplation (III.8), each product being a successively lower image of its maker or cause, but all, even the lowest, depending on the first cause.

1, 1–4 This opening sentence refers to the concluding two chapters of III.8 *On Contemplation*, for contemplation leads to Intellect and the source and cause of Intellect, "that which is simply one" (III.8.10, 22) which is identified with the Good

(III.8.12). The topic of beauty, the beauty of the universe and of its intelligible archetype is also introduced in this final chapter (III.8.11, 26f.). It is the combination of these two themes, Intellect and beauty, which provides the starting point of the present discussion: how can we contemplate the beauty of Intellect? Although the way we do this (initially through the contemplation of physical beauty) may recall his earlier treatise I.6 *On Beauty,* he is more concerned in the present treatise with the nature of Intellect itself (and its consequences for the status and value of the physical universe) than with Intellect as the goal of our own spiritual journey. The initial question with its stress on "how" disguises the fact that discovering the nature of intelligible beauty through philosophical reflection is intrinsically connected with our personal apprehension of, and thus unity with, it.

1, 2 *true intellect*: The description of intellect here as "true" serves to emphasize that he is dealing with intellect at its highest level at which intellect and object of thought are one (as analyzed in V.5). For Plotinus sometimes uses the term "intellect" more loosely of the activity of soul at the higher levels of discursive thought (e.g., VI.2.7, 40).

1, 3 The "father" of Intellect is the One, which "transcends" it. The phraseology recalls the Good which "transcends being" in Plato *Republic* 509b9.

1, 5 *insofar as it is possible to express such matters*: Plotinus is, perhaps, thinking here of *Phaedrus* 247c3–5, where Plato says that no poet has yet or ever will succeed in hymning the praises of the intelligible universe. Of course it is to this very level of reality, of which Plato leaves such a vague account, that Plotinus devotes so much attention and intricate analysis, not least in this treatise. And yet he still frequently refers to the limitations of human speech and rational thought to express adequately the nature of the intelligible realm, which is fully accessible only to intellect, the cognitive level above that of discursive thought, spatial and temporal distinctions, and logical sequence. This problem is later picked up in the analogy with gold at 3, 11f. and in the comparison with hieroglyphics in Chapter 6. Rational discourse is, however, an indispensable instrument in the ascent to intellectual vision and for its communication to our understanding. The ultimate inaccessibility of intellect to discursive expression also supplies Plotinus with a motive for employing myth, and particularly Platonic myth (e.g., the extensive reference to the *Phaedrus* myth in this treatise) as a means of communicating transcendent metaphysical truths. See further the note at 12, 3f. on myth.

1, 10 Statues of the Graces and the Muses were quite commonplace. Plotinus may also have been aware of the sort of allegorization of the Graces to which the Stoic philosopher Chrysippus dedicated a whole book according to Seneca (*On Benefits* I.3). And Diogenes Laertius tells us (*Lives of the Philosophers*, IV.1) that Plato dedicated a shrine to the

Muses in the Academy grove, to which Speusippus later added statues of the Graces.

1, 16 *in the one who thought it*: Not in the sense that it is a fabrication of the artist. The artist's concept is itself an objectively existing form, as we see from the following words: "this beauty was, therefore, in art." In this respect the beauty of artistic creations, in the end, depends, as does the beauty of natural things, on the same level of objective causes, the transcendent forms of the intelligible world.

1, 18 *share*: Greek *metechein* is the Platonic expression for the participation of sensibles in forms. Here it is applied to the participation of the artist in the form of beauty, which lies above him.

1, 20 *another*: It is made absolutely clear that beauty in the artist's mind, whether seen as a form or *logos,* is not identical with the beauty in art, that is, beauty at the higher intelligible level. The beauty found in the statue is lower still. The concept of entities producing something below them whilst they themselves *remain* is an essential component of Plotinus' metaphysics whether expressed in terms of the hypostases, which "produce" each other whilst not losing their own integrity ("remaining"), or of the unfolding of forms as *logoi* at descending levels.

The term *logos* seems to be often identical with form (*eidos*). *Logos* is translated here as "rational principle" and stresses more the notion of the abstract formula than the shaping factor in *eidos*. To the extent that it has connotations of the discursive from its connection with "word" and "speech" and its implication being "expressive" of something more original and therefore secondary, it is not commonly used to indicate form at the level of intellect, but rather the evolving levels of form at successively lower levels of reality.

See also V.9.5, where he refers to this "remaining" of the transcendent form, and to natural and artistic creation: "The objects of sense are what they are called by participation, since their underlying nature receives its shape from elsewhere: bronze, for instance, from the art of sculpture and wood from the art of carpentry, the art passing into them through an image, but itself remaining in self-identity outside matter and possessing the true statue or bed." The "true bed" is a reference to Plato *Republic* X.597c3 where Plato argues that the artist, when producing a picture of a bed looks not to the transcendent form of bed but merely to its image, the physical bed, to conclude that the artistic product is at a third remove from reality. But Plotinus adopts a more positive view of the artist and appears either to ignore Plato's conclusion or to interpret it differently. He may, for example, have considered it to be applicable only to lower artistic genres. Proclus managed to avoid Plato's strictures on "immoral" myths by arguing that they could be employed by the philosopher who was able to understand their hidden meaning.

1, 22 *only so far as the stone yielded to art*: The suitability (*epitēdeiotēs*) of a substrate to receive form or powers is a constant theme in Plotinus and runs parallel with the idea that powers diminish as they descend from the highest to the lowest levels. The two may be seen in this paragraph where just a little later he speaks of the diminishing power of levels of beauty as an example of a more general principle. These two principles provide Plotinus with an explanation for the imperfections of this world compared with its transcendent model. But an immediate problem with matter as a restrictive component is that it seems to provide it with a positive force of obstruction whereas he is elsewhere (see II.4.13–14) concerned to remove all qualities from matter.

1, 23 *if art makes*: By making "art" here the subject rather than the artist Plotinus wants to stress that the idea in the artist's mind is more important than the physical effort of creation. Thus in the previous lines he has said that the artist makes because he shares in art and not by eyes and hands.

what it itself is: He is already pre-empting the key idea which is expressed later (9, 35–42) that beauty and being are identical in the intelligible world.

1, 26ff. Degrees of unity are paralleled by degrees of power and reality in a world that becomes increasingly more pluralized as it unfolds, until it projects itself three-dimensionally in matter.

1, 31–32 *For it is not lack of music*: this seems an odd way of summarizing the principle enunciated in the previous lines, that powers diminish. Perhaps Plotinus wants to stress that the inferiority of music in the sensible world compared to that of the intelligible world (and the music of the spheres) is not primarily caused by the imperfections of sensible media but rather the diminishing power of music as it descends to lower levels from its transcendent cause. This would suggest, then, a correction to the initial reference (line 22) to the apparent recalcitrance of the physical medium (of stone).

1, 32–40 We may immediately think of Plato's criticism in *Republic* X 597bff. of imitation in art. But would Plotinus have criticized Plato so directly? Plotinus regarded himself as a Platonist and placed Plato as the focal point and supreme exponent of what he regarded as a single definitive philosophical system, one which still needed clarification (see V.1.8, 10–14) but which should not contradict it (VI.4.16, 4–7), although he does seem to leave room for debate (II.9.6, 43–52). Rist (1967, 183–187) thinks his view on imitation is a direct criticism of Plato, Armstrong (1974, 179) that he was probably not fully aware that he was contradicting Plato. On balance it seems more likely that he here has in mind those who, in his view, have misinterpreted the Platonic text. The notion that the artist has direct access to the intelligible model can be traced back at least to the first century BCE (Cicero *Orator* 8–10; Seneca *Letters* 65, 7–10; Alcinous, *The Handbook of*

Platonism 163, 21–23; Philostratos *Life of Apollonius* VI.19.2; and see the discussion in Theiler [1934, 15ff.]).

1, 34 *natural things too imitate other things*: That is, the whole of the physical universe is an imitation of its intelligible model, an idea to which Plotinus returns in vivid terms in Chapter 4.

1, 37 *on their own initiative*: Not only does the artist go back to the perfect intelligible form of man but adds something. This is a remarkable tribute to the creative genius of the artist. A similar idea in the general production of nature may be seen in VI.7.9, 40–46 where he describes the unfolding of the form of horse from its intelligible model to its final physical manifestation. At this final stage additional elements (e.g., nails and horn) develop to compensate for the deficiencies experienced in the progressive diminution in power of the unfolding form.

Chapter 2

The enquiry now moves to the cause of beauty in natural physical phenomena. The origin of their beauty, as in the case of the beauty of works of art, will also be found in transcendent form. He argues that if the experience of beauty does not come from the externality or mass of an object it must come from something immaterial. We then add to this that nature or "logos," the producing agent, must itself be beautiful. This then leads to the examination in the next chapter of the various manifestations of "logos" or "rational principle" at different levels of reality.

2, 2f. The list of beautiful physical objects needs some explaining. It is rather surprising that he introduces gods and goddesses and even more so those that are not visible. But their relevance will become apparent with the introduction of the *Phaedrus* myth in Chapter 4. Also surprising in this initial list is that it is limited to "creatures" (*zōa* living beings, whether "rational" i.e., men or "irrational" i.e., animals), since it is implied in 1, 13–14 that a stone can be beautiful as stone. From a later treatise (VI.7 [38]) we may infer that

Plotinus could have expanded the range to include things and processes which we would regard as totally inanimate; for in arguing that the intelligible world has the patterns of everything within it including plants he concludes "the growth, then, and the shaping of stones and the inner patterning of mountains as they grow one must most certainly suppose take place because an ensouled forming principle is working within them and giving them form; and this is the active form of the earth, like what is called the growth-nature in trees." (VI.7.10, 24–28). It is then probable that the restriction to "living beings" in our passage is due to its close connection with III.8; it was relatively easy for Plotinus to slot living being into the schema of different levels of contemplation envisaged there. For even the most basic living beings and life forms possess some rudimentary kind of cognitive activity.

2, 7 In rejecting purely material principles as responsible for structuring bodies he may here have Aristotle in mind, who in *Parts of Animals* 651a14–15 makes blood the ultimate nourishment and matter for bodies and in *Generation of animals* 729a32 equates the menstrual fluids with "primary matter."

He then goes on to reject as insufficient conventional explanations of beauty such as color and shape as in I.6.1, 20f. The following sentence reduces the choices to nothing, something without shape, or "something simple like that which circumscribes" (the Greek is *to periechon* "that which contains"). The first is clearly inadmissible, the absence of shape suggests the incorporeal in general (see Plato *Phaedrus* 247c6–7 where true being has neither color nor shape—"*aschēmatistos*"), whereas "something simple like that which circumscribes" suggests an incorporeal power such as soul (see IV.3.20, 25 where soul contains [*periechon*] rather than is contained), indicating here something which has the power to impose limit or shape of some kind, but is itself simple, that is, incorporeal since it is without shape which is a characteristic of body. This is all leading up to the identification of the cause of beauty as an active power, i.e., form in line 14.

The Greek here is not easy and seems to be corrupt. Armstrong translates: "rather the color of these [blood and menstrual fluid] is different and their shape is either no shape or a shapeless shape or like that which delimits something simple." I have taken it in the same way as Laurent.

2, 12–14 By visible gods he is probably referring to the stars (see III.2.14, 25–30 and II.9.5, 4–14) and by the gods which are not visible but whose beauty can be seen, he may mean the gods of traditional mythology whose form is sometimes revealed to men in theophanies or in works of art (such as Pheidias' statue of Zeus mentioned later) and in literature.

2, 19–20 *insofar as it is mass*: That is, when taken without any consideration of even the most basic form imposed on it. The bare stone, for example, in Chapter 1 already displays form in its shape, color, and texture. Mass (*ongkos*) is what is "prior" to this. It differs, too, from matter in that it represents for Plotinus the three-dimensionality which is the contribution of pure matter to the constitution of physical objects, that is, the mode in which the immanent forms express themselves in matter.

If mass (or indeed matter) were said to be beautiful, we would be designating as beautiful something that was in itself devoid of form and thereby excluding rational principle which is the provider of form as a cause of beauty.

It is clear from the following lines that Plotinus does not regard the magnitude of objects and their physicality, for example their resistance, as the product of form, but rather as characteristics of mass. What gives shape and beauty to objects is their immanent form and it is this form that we perceive rather than the mass of the object. Even size is not perceived by us as the mass-size of an object but its size as a form (2, 27–28).

2, 25 *while something is outside us*: An object that has not yet impinged upon and transmitted itself to our sense organs.

2, 27–28 *But the size too is brought in with it . . . . large in form*: This indicates that the object as perceived, although entirely constituted of forms, is perceived *as an object with physical properties* and is thus different from the ideal which is without such manifested physical properties.

2, 29 *the maker*: The argument now moves from form to the maker. Form, maker, rational principle (see note on 3, 3–4) are different aspects of the creative power that originates from the One and is manifested most fully at the level of Intellect. Sometimes Plotinus wants to distinguish these different aspects while still maintaining their essential unity. And so in this passage the discussion moves from rational principle and form to the maker in line 29.

2, 31 *nature*: Sometimes "nature" (e.g., in III.8) is given almost the status of a hypostasis, on a level just beneath that of the world soul. But here it refers to the rational principle which produces the physical world and the term "nature" simply reminds us that the subject of the chapter is the natural world as opposed to the products of art.

2, 35 *pursue an image of himself*: See the example of Narcissus in I.6.8, 8–12.

2, 40 *his inner beauty*: For example, Socrates, who is visually ugly but beautiful within (see Alcibiades' speech in Plato *Symposium* 215bf.).

2, 41–46 See I.6.9, 29f. for the idea that like is perceived by like, that you must make yourself beautiful in order to see both beauty outside and true beauty.

2, 46 A prerequisite for all philosophical endeavor is a morally ordered life. The Neoplatonists promoted this theoretical requirement by introductions to philosophy, commentaries on the *Ethics* of Aristotle or the works of Epictetus and, not least, by works such as the lives of Pythagoras which presented a model for the philosophical life of virtue.

Before proceeding to the study of the different levels of "rational principles" we are encouraged to purify our inner selves in order to make our intellects receptive. See V.1.1. for this purification which begins with a turning away from externals and a realization of the nature and worth of the soul. It is at once a spiritual and an intellectual exercise.

Chapter 3

He now wants to lead us on to an apprehension of intelligible beauty and of the intelligible world as a whole which is based on more than reasoning: that is, it is based on the direct vision of our intellects which can be one with the universal Intellect. The chapter concludes with a description of the intelligible world which suggests the experience of mystical vision with its portrayal of a world of mutually interpenetrating realities, but which is also conceived in the discursively grounded understanding of the relationship of parts to wholes. The following chapter explores this world further.

3, 3–4 *the rational principle in the soul of the good man*: Plotinus likes to use the term *logos,* translated here as "rational principle" as an equivalent of Platonic "form" (see 1, 24; 36; 2, 17). It has the advantage of avoiding the physical connotations of the expressions used for "form" (*eidos, morphē*) and of suggesting more the notion of a rational formula (a sort of DNA) which constitutes an entity (the word *logos* is also used by him for "reason" or "discursive thought"). It is frequently, as in this passage, applied to successive levels of reality, each being, as it were, an "expression" (*logos* as "word") or image of its prior. This is the case here, where he distinguishes "rational principle" at the level of embodiment, above this, its cause, at the level of nature, higher still at the level of soul, and then at the level of the soul of the good man. The causal force of *logos* can also be equated with productive power or "the maker," again at different levels.

But why does he distinguish soul and the soul of the good man? The only candidate for the former is the world soul, for it can hardly mean the hypostasis Soul, which is to be placed at the highest level, immediately after Intellect. Now he often cites the world soul as a psychic level to which humans can aspire (see Chapter 7, 28–35), but here, in putting the human soul at a higher level ("clearest of all is the rational principle in the soul of the good man"), it seems likely that he is thinking of that very highest "part" of the human soul that provides the link between the realm of discursive reason and that of intellect. For it is the intelligible world and our experience of it that forms the central subject of this treatise. For this highest aspect or undescended soul see note on 10, 20–22.

This passage is also one of the many occasions within the treatise when he adverts to the personal experience of the intelligible universe which is reserved for the philosopher (the good man).

3, 6 *it has brought order to the soul*: A distinction is made between soul and its "rational principle" which is said to bring light to the soul from a higher light (intellect). The "rational principles" that the soul receives from intellect have the double function of forming soul as soul and providing it with the rational content of its discursive reason, which it then transmits to the lower faculties. But, as Plotinus makes clear, the cause (intellect) of these rational principles in soul is itself not a rational principle because it entirely transcends them. In II.4.5, 8, however, Plotinus, more loosely, calls intellect a rational principle.

We note here equation of "rational principle" with light. See II.4.5, 7–8 where "rational principle" is also identified with light. We can speak of a metaphysics of light in Plotinus because of the important role it plays as more than a metaphor. This all begins with Plato's analogy of the sun and the Good in *Republic* 508bf. But in claiming that light is itself incorporeal Plotinus transforms what is an analogy in Plato to a reality. Light is equated with the power of production, which is emitted from the One and transmitted through Intellect and Soul down throughout the entire universe. See Beierwaltes 1961; Smith (2011^2, 14–19).

3, 10 *the intellect which operates always and not intermittently*: The concept of an ever-active intellect goes back to Aristotle, whose thought, as expressed especially in *Metaphysics* 6 1071b12–23 and 1074b15ff., he creatively grafted onto Plato's theory of Forms. The two essential ideas are: 1. The divine intellect must always be exercising its thinking, that is, always actually and never potentially thinking, and 2. Since the essence of the divine is thinking and the object of its thought cannot be anything inferior to itself, its thinking is a thinking of thinking. Plotinus then identifies the Platonic Forms not only as the object of Intellect, the divine mind, but as identical with the divine mind itself. This is done by identifying the objects of thought with the thinker (Intellect) through their shared *activity* which is the essence of each. The argument is set out in its most complex form in V.3.5, 41–44: "If then Intellect is activity and its substance is activity, it is one and the same with its activity; but being and the intelligible are also one with activity. All together are one, intellect, intellection, the intelligible." The conversion of the rather statically conceived Platonic Forms into active intellects is one of the boldest and richest concepts in Plotinus' analysis of Intellect.

3, 12–13 *the image must come from intellect. . . . not conceive of it by means of an image*: An implicit warning about the inadequacies of analogies and an encouragement to rise above them. Plotinus frequently does use images in the form of analogies to make inferences from a lower ("inferior") level of reality about the nature of what is above, one level of reality being an "image" of the other, what one might call metaphysical analogies. He now wants us to have an image that, paradoxically, is not an image, that is, an intellectual picture (image) that is not a subordinate copy but the object itself. And so he takes the bold step of urging us to go beyond discursive reason (indicated by the word "conclude" in line 6), where we make inferences, to apprehend Intellect, and thus intelligible beauty, at its own level by means of our own individual intellect. The point of the gold analogy is precisely that the individual piece of gold is just as much gold as any other piece of the ingot or, indeed, of the entire ingot. That is, our intellect is identical with universal Intellect and thus able to grasp it in the fullest sense. To find our intellect we must "purify" ourselves by deed (moral activity) and word (refining our discursive reasoning) until we finally attain pure intellectual activity.

Although the gold analogy is still taken from an "inferior" level of reality than the nature of intellect which it is intended to elucidate, it is applied to intellect in a purely *illustrative* way, unlike the case of metaphysical analogies in which there is a causal link between activities at different levels in the structure of the universe. More generally on analogy see Smith 2011[2].

3, 17f. The introduction of gods into the argument at first sight seems rather odd. But the challenge announced earlier of finding some image to communicate the notion of the intelligible world has called to mind Plato's vivid description of just such a world, resplendent with divine beings, in *Phaedrus* 247, as we see in the following paragraphs. Plotinus may also have recalled the phrase "immense beauty" not only from *Republic* (referring to the Good) but also from *Symposium*

218e2 where it refers to the inner beauty of Socrates. Thus he may be combining the notion of the inner beauty of our intellect and that of the gods. Moreover Plotinus has a particular interest in the divinity of stars to which as ensouled celestial phenomena he assigns a role in the governance of the universe. On several occasions (for example, Chapter 7, 28–35 of this treatise) he refers to the possibility that human individuals, when they return in contemplation of Intellect, may share with the world soul in the governance of the universe, thus combining and reconciling their practical (embodied) and contemplative functions. In this sense the intra-mundane gods in particular ("the gods in the heavens" [3, 28]) are models for human imitation.

3, 21 *visible*: Not in a physical but in an intellectual sense as in line 27 "Intellect sees."

3, 22 *those who have bodies*: Plotinus may be recalling *Phaedrus* 246c7–d1, where Plato is thinking of the Greek conception of the gods as anthropomorphic. "Our fancy pictures the god whom we have never seen, nor fully conceived, as an immortal living being, possessed of a body and soul." But it is as likely that he means the astral gods. In III.5.6, 21–23 he refers to "visible gods" which he locates down to the level of the moon and which are designated as "secondary gods" after the "intelligible gods." Plotinus may also here be alluding to the traditional linking of contemplation with observing the wonderful order of the heavens (cf. Philo, *On the Creation of the World* 54; Cicero, *On the Nature of the Gods* II 153). This may also be seen as confirmation of Plotinus' concern to counter the Gnostic demotion of the physical world and the heavenly bodies, as he does explicitly in II.9.18, 30f. in the context of star souls.

3, 25 *always mentally active*: See on 3,10 above.

3, 27 *the gods in the heavens*: That is, the celestial gods, who are on the same level as the soul of the good man who has learnt to rule his body with ease, before rising to the next level of the gods in the intelligible world.

3, 29 *that heaven*: The intelligible world, the archetype of the physical heavens (and universe).

3, 32f. A remarkably vivid representation of the intelligible universe where everything is in a sense everything else, that is, a world of interpenetrating realities, often compared by Plotinus to the original "mixture" of Anaxagoras and, more discursively, with the relationship of geometrical theorems or mathematical formulae, each of which is in a sense all because each implies the totality of theorems, whilst maintaining at the same time its particular individual contribution (V.9.6, 3f.; 8, 1f.; IV.9.5, 18).

3, 34–35 *do not despise men or any of the other things there*: That is, heaven, earth, sea, living creatures, etc. He has in mind here the Gnostic demotion ("despise") of the physical universe. It is just because this physical universe and its inhabitants have their origins in the intelligible world, where the gods contemplate them, that we should not despise them. For they are an integral part of the intelligible whole ("they belong there"). This does not contradict the previous comment (line 26) that the gods are not acquainted with "human concerns"; for it is the transcendent and integral totality rather than the separated details that they contemplate. And it is the same level that we too can attain when we become more than "human."

Chapter 4

This chapter continues the analysis of the intelligible universe by employing a number of common metaphysical concepts (predominant features, identity of substrate and its characteristic nature), concluding with its identity with "wisdom," which is to be understood as something higher than discursive reason. He is insistent that the "forms" of the intelligible world are realities and not mere propositions. It is the task of the philosopher, the lover of wisdom, to explore their nature.

4, 1 *"easy life"*: Homer *Iliad* 6.138, referring to the life of the gods.

4, 2–3 *truth is their mother, nurse, being and nourishment*: See I.3.4, 10–12 where the activity of dialectic finds its culmination in "the world of intellect" where "it occupies itself, casting off falsehood and feeding the soul in what Plato calls 'the plain of truth.'" The images are suggested by Plato's description of the transcendent world in *Phaedrus* 247d: "Even as the mind of a god is nourished by reason and knowledge, so also is it with every soul that has a care to receive her proper food."

For "truth" see the same passage: "Our discourse is upon truth" (247c5–6), "the plain of truth" (248b6), and for the link between "truth" and "being" see 247c7: "It is there that real being dwells," a link which Plotinus explores elsewhere (e.g., V.5.1–2; III.7.4, 1–8).

4, 5–36 Plotinus continues to take his inspiration from the *Phaedrus* passage in which Plato describes the life of the gods. This now leads him to consider the relationship between thinker and object of thought.

4, 6 *light is transparent to light*: Thinker and object of thought are at once distinct and yet identical. See V.3.8, 20f. for further elaboration of this double function of light in the intelligible world: "Sight, since it is light, or rather united with light, sees light: for its sees colors; but in the intelligible world seeing is not through another [medium], but through itself, because it is not directed outside. Intellect therefore sees one light with another, not through another. Light then sees another light: it therefore itself sees itself. And this light shining in the soul illuminates it; that is, it makes it intelligent; that is, it makes it like itself, the light above. For if you consider that it is like the trace of light that comes to be in the soul and still more beautiful and greater and clearer, you will come near to the nature of Intellect and the intelligible." The same point is being made here, that at the level of intellect thinker and object of thought are identical ("itself sees itself") and at the same time in another sense distinct ("light sees another light"). The light here in question is an incorporeal metaphysical light. See on 3, 6 above.

4, 11 *stands out in each*: The concept of determining the identity of something by its predominant features begins with Anaxagoras' explanation of physical change in which each thing contains everything else (fr. 11) but takes its particular characterization from what predominates. The idea is transposed by Plotinus from the material level to the incorporeal intelligible world. See Stamatellos (2007, 147–150).

4, 12f. The co-existence of movement and rest, which is so evident in his vivid descriptions of the intelligible world in this and the previous chapter, takes its rise from the so-called five *genera* or categories of the intelligible world Plotinus extracted from Plato's *Sophist* 258f.: movement, rest, sameness, difference, and being. One of Plotinus' key ideas is that the Intelligible World may be analyzed in terms of these five fundamental categories. They may be conceived as being essential aspects of intelligible reality. In Intellect we have both "movement" because intellect is an activity, the activity of thinking, and "rest" for it is always in possession of the object of its thinking. Intellect, too, is both identical with the object of its thinking and may also be distinguished from it. Similarly, the thought content of Intellect is both plural—the many different Forms—and one—expressing the unity and coherence of the whole in which each part is also in a sense both itself and the whole. These four genera thus express the complex diversity in unity of the intelligible world. We then must finally add "being," for the intelligible world as well as each of its elements is what really exists as opposed to the physical world, which is a world of becoming.

4, 15–19 In the intelligible world everything is substance or being (*ousia*). Even so-called essential differentiations are identical in each case with a thing's substance or being. Thus Beauty is not beautiful because of the presence of beauty in something that does not possess beauty in itself. This critique of Aristotle's doctrine of substance is fully explored in II.6 [17] and elaborated in VI.1–3 [42–44].

4, 17 *when it ascends, as it were*: The word "ascends" suggests that Plotinus is, perhaps, thinking here almost ("as it were") of a hierarchy within the intelligible world in the context of the relationship of Forms to each other.

4, 19 *it is as if one were to think*: We might imagine that the light in the heavens originated with the stars themselves and that would be like the intelligible world where everything is all together and the essence of each individual part (a luminous star) is identical with its being; but in fact the physical heavens are not like that since the light of the stars is not its own but taken from another source.

4, 21 *one part would come from another part*: That is, parts are not products of a whole but of something which is itself only a part, presumably because nothing in the physical world is a perfect whole, but the different parts contribute toward the being of each other (e.g., the stars have their light from another part of the heavens). This is contrasted with the intelligible world, which is whole as Being.

In lines 21–2 the text has *oun ouk ek merous . . . allou* "*not* (*ouk*) from another part" but I have deleted the negative with Vitringa and Theiler. The insertion of a negative (*ou* or *ouk*) would be an easy error with the eye moving from *ou* in *oun* ("then") to the *k* of *ek*. If we do leave the negative we would have to fill out the translation of the sentence to mean "in this world one part would not come out of another *identical* part," that is, in this world parts are not identical with the whole whereas in the intelligible world the part is both a part and identical with the whole. Even a piece of gold, though identical generically with the whole piece of gold, is numerically (in this case in mass) distinct. This is possible, but Plotinus' stress with "*allo allou*" is on the otherness rather than the identity of the part.

4, 25 Lynceus was one of the Argonauts who was so sharp-sighted that he could see through the earth. See Apollonius Rhodius I.151–5; Plato, *Letter* VII 344a1; Aristotle, *On Generation and Corruption* 328a15.

4, 27f. The unwearied life of contemplation may be contrasted with the troubled life of human souls as described in Plato's *Phaedrus* 248a6–b5. See also Plato, *Philebus* 35b for the analysis of desire in terms of filling and emptying and I.8.8, 6 and VI.8.3, 13. In III.5.9, Plotinus interprets the story of Poros and Penia (Plenty and Poverty) as representing the unfulfilled nature of the soul's ascent to the divine. Love (the desire of the soul for the Good) has a mixed nature from his birth from Plenty and Poverty: "Need, in that he wishes to be filled, but not without a share in plenitude, in that he seeks what is wanting to that which he already has. . . . the lack and the aspiration and the memory of the rational principles coming together in the soul, produced the activity directed towards the Good, and this is Love."

4, 36 *life is wisdom*: "Life" for Plotinus may refer to the life in a living body or the life of, and provided by, soul. In the end all life is a form of intellection or rather contemplation, seen at different levels. This is one of the main points to emerge from the preceding treatise III.8. See particularly III.8.8, 17: "All life is a kind of thinking." It is in this sense that life is said here to be wisdom. The context of this passage also demands that life here is life at its highest level, that of intellect. "Wisdom" is also suggested by the role of the "philosopher" or "lover of wisdom" in *Phaedrus* 249a1–2, c4 and 248d3, and perhaps by the pre-eminent importance amongst the cardinal virtues of "wisdom" in Stoic theory; for it is the Stoics whom Plotinus has in mind in the next chapter.

The argument moves from the general premise that all life is a form of thinking (wisdom) to the identification of the life in the intelligible world as the first and highest form of life, that is, intellection. Intellection proper (wisdom at the highest level) excludes the imperfections implied in discursive thought and is identical with being.

4, 49 *But we have not reached an understanding of it*: The wisdom that brings a true apprehension of beauty lies above discursive reason and thus beyond normal logic. See VI.7.33, 1–7 for removing from our apprehension of beauty all spatial features and then all logical distinctions, "the shape in reasoning": "Therefore, even when it [the intelligible world] is called beauty, one must even more avoid shape of this kind; but it must not be set before the eyes, that you may not fall out of beauty into what is called beauty by obscure participation. But the shapeless form is beautiful, since it is form, and is so in proportion to the length you go in stripping all shape from it, the shape in reasoning, for instance, by which we say that one form differs from another, as we say that justice and moral probity are different from each other, although they are beautiful."

For the task of the Platonist as a creative interpreter of Plato see also V.1.8, 10–14.

Chapter 5

The first nine lines of the chapter summarize the conclusion already reached in Chapters 1 to 3 with the addition of two points: that the intelligible model is conceived as "wisdom" (sophia) and the productive activity of the individual (the artist here) is itself subsumed under the universal (here the "natural") intelligible model or "wisdom." This is not a compound constructed of separately existing parts but a really existent whole that is at the same time multiple. He then goes on to reject by implication an ascending series of candidates for the ultimate source of this "wisdom": it will be found to be neither nature, nor soul, but intellect whose being is identical with "wisdom."

He has now established that the object or content of transcendent "wisdom" is something real, that is, true being, and not abstractions or axioms. The following chapter pursues this point further.

5, 1–6 If wisdom is the ultimate cause of both natural and crafted phenomena, and art looks back to this ultimate wisdom (as we have seen in Chapter 1), then the artist who is himself a natural product and thus caused by this wisdom is active by this very same wisdom. The prominence given here to the possibility of the individual activating an intellect (his own) which shares in the integrity and wholeness of universal Intellect recurs throughout this treatise even though its main emphasis is on the universal rather than the particular intellect.

5, 3 *if someone*: For example, an artist as described in Chapter 1. Theiler takes *tis* (some, someone) as referring back to wisdom in line 1.

5, 5 *by which he has himself come into being*: This may refer in a restricted sense to the fact that the artist as a human being is simply part of the natural order. I have interpreted it in the broader sense that it includes the whole of the individual up to the level of intellect. This seems to be confirmed by his reference here to the craftsman or artist, who, in Chapter 1, is said to look in his creative activity to the transcendent form ("wisdom itself") and by the identification of the craftsman's wisdom with "the wisdom which is whole as one" (lines 6ff.).

5, 8 *the primary wisdom*: That is, Intellect itself as established in 4, 38.

5, 9f. The argument here seems difficult to follow if we understand "nature" ("natural") in line 5 as having exactly the same range of meaning as "nature" in line 10; for there would then seem to be a contradiction between what is accepted in a positive way in the first paragraph (up to line 9) and what is clearly rejected as inadequate in lines 9f. But there is, in fact, a difference in the range of meaning. In line 5 he is concerned with overcoming the difference between art and nature by claiming that even art is something that is brought about through an agent, the artist, who is himself a member of the natural order; and so the wisdom he attains and employs is one that is, in the end, a wisdom of the natural order in the same sense in which soul and intellect are "natures." The imagined objectors of lines 9 onward are proposing a kind of wisdom that is found "in nature," in the restricted sense of the physical world in which we find ourselves.

5, 9 *But if they say*: He is probably here thinking of the Stoics, who identified Zeus as the wisdom and rational order of the universe with the universe itself. In V.9.1, 10–16 he criticizes them for not rising beyond the level of corporeal reality. His interrogation of the Stoics continues: a Stoic might well contend that the *logos* comes from the world soul or from Zeus as intellect. Plotinus' procedure here is to imagine a discussion with Stoics that eventually leads to his own view that the ultimate source is Intellect, but an Intellect that transcends the physical universe and whose wisdom is identical with its being.

5, 11 *from another*: He is probably thinking of Soul, which would be next in his normal hierarchy. In Stoic terms this would be the Cosmic Soul.

5, 14 *that is impossible unless it is itself intellect*: This is, of course, the conclusion that Plotinus wants, as the next sentence makes clear.

5, 15 *true*: The term "true" as applied to the intelligible world is derived from Plato, for example *Phaedrus* 247c8; d4; *Republic* 509a6; and 517c4. For Plotinus "true" indicates that a thing's being and essence is identical, that is, it is self-contained, the situation that obtains at the level of intellect. See the discussion of "truth" at the level of intellect in V.5.1 and 2. For the identity of wisdom and being see the note on 3, 10 on the identity of Intellect with its objects (Being) through their shared activity of intellection. The mutual and dynamic interdependence of the different aspects of the intelligible world is expressed in these lines. That being has its origin in wisdom might, at first, suggest that Plotinus is abandoning the Platonic theory that the Forms are not simply ideas produced by the mind but objectively existing realities. But Plotinus can say that the objects of intellect are in a sense the product of intellect because he excludes all temporal notions at this level. In VI.6.6, 8–10 and elsewhere he does in fact stress the priority of being. But his more nuanced position, whilst allowing with Plato that being is prior to thought, effectively avoids the issue by identifying the two: "If then Intellect was thought of as preceding Being, we should have to say that Intellect by coming to actuality in its thinking perfected and produced real beings; but since we must think of Being as preceding Intellect, we must assume that the real beings have their place in the thinking subject, and that the actuality of thinking is in the real beings. . . . But Being is actuality; so both have one actuality, or rather both are one thing. Being and Intellect are therefore one nature (V.9.8, 8f.).

5, 17 *beings which do not possess wisdom*: Anything on a lower level than intelligible being; this would presumably include human individuals at the level of discursive reason, which is below the level of intellect which constitutes "true" wisdom.

5, 21 *exceedingly happy (hypereudaimones)*: The word is found in Aristotle, *Rhetoric* 1385b21 and Lucian *Gallus* 20.

5, 22 *beautiful images*: He probably has in mind Alcibiades who, in Plato *Symposium* 215b1–3, 216e6–217a1 praises the wonderful images (*agalmata*) underlying Socrates' ugly exterior.

5, 23 *not images (agalmata) that are drawn*: He has perhaps already in mind the analogy of Egyptian pictograms with which the next chapter commences.

5, 24–25 A realist interpretation of Plato's Forms, as objectively existing entities, founded on texts such as Plato *Republic* 507b, 509b as opposed to interpretations of them as logical propositions or abstract concepts. In deference to normal English phraseology I have translated the Greek *onta* and *ousias* as "realities" (lit. "things that are") and "substances," although elsewhere I have rendered *ousia* as being(s).

Chapter 6

Beginning with the comparison of intelligibles to Egyptian pictograms, he then lists the modes of discursive reasoning which "wisdom" transcends, before turning to the way in which it is in fact communicated to discursive reasoning.

6, 5 *by engraving images*: He is probably thinking of the pure pictograms used in temples rather than the characters of partially alphabetic hieroglyphic texts. This is brought out by the word translated here as "image" (*agalma)* which can mean a statue or portrait. See on 5, 22–23. The word is used frequently by Plotinus, as here, for the intelligibles and thus does not contain the notion of copy as in other expressions for image, such as *eidolon, ichnos,* or *eikon.*

6, 4–5 "Words and propositions" are the written expression of letters, "sounds and the utterance of axioms" are their oral expression. Plotinus wants to exclude both written and spoken expression from intellection. It is also possible that he uses the most basic expression "sounds" to indicate non-articulated forms of speech, as for example magical utterances that are sounds rather than words.

6, 8–9 *substrate*: The word *hypokeimenon* may sometimes indicate "matter" in a physical context, but also, as here, matter in the intelligible world, which, on the analogy of substrate in the physical world, is the supporter, carrier—or, better—enabler of Form. In the intelligible world, however, matter and form are ultimately identical. Hence here we have the additional designation *athroon* "all together at once." This complex of ideas has already appeared in 4, 18–19.

6, 10 *secondary image*: Having translated *agalma*, which literally means a statue as "image," but not, of course, image in the sense of something derived from an original, it is now necessary to distinguish the word *eidolon*, which does imply the notion of a copy.

6, 12 *lays open*: I have interpreted *exeuriskon* as a participle agreeing with "secondary image" which I take to be the object of the verb "knows" (*oide*, line 13). Theiler and Laurent interpret this in a similar way. Armstrong and others take *exeuriskon* as a third person plural verb and translate "they find." But this leaves us asking who "they" are.

6, 14–15 This later image of wisdom may be identified with what Plotinus elsewhere calls *logoi*, the pluralized and deployed manifestations of the transcendent forms or *noeta*. Unlike their transcendent originals they do not contain *in themselves*, that is, identical with themselves, the original causative force, which it is, however, their function to transmit to the physical world.

6, 15 *For this reason*: Because we realize that the immanent causes of the universe are insufficient to explain its wonderful appearance (lines 12–15), we are led to posit a more perfect set of causes.

6, 16 *to be necessarily like this*: We are unable through discursive reason to make a necessary statement about the nature of the intelligible world. This implies that any statements we do make about it are provisional in the sense of conditioned by the restrictions imposed by the nature of discursive thought, which is the implication of the phrase "scarcely or not at all . . . revealed by research." Only when we are ourselves employing intellect and operating at the level of intellect can we be said to have full knowledge of that world. This double approach, through discursive reason and the direct vision of intellect, is illustrated further by the thought experiment in Chapter 9.

Chapter 7

He now takes the physical universe as a whole as an example of how ordered planning is a result rather than the cause of the ordered product. The principle involved here leads Plotinus to "demythologize" the Platonic demiurge of the Timaeus who is described as though planning the universe. In fact what produces the universe is prior to all planning and reasoning.

7, 1–12 For another statement and application (to virtue) of the principle applied here see I.2.1, 43–45: "The perceptible house is not the same thing as the intelligible house, though it is made in its likeness; the perceptible house participates in arrangement and order, but in the intelligible world, in its rational principle, there is no arrangement or order or proportion," for these are the result of discursive reason's unravelling and expressing in discrete form what, in the intelligible world, is a continuous whole, "substrate and all together at once"; in fact a "laying open of the causes."

7, 9–10 *where would it . . . such things?*: If we ascribe discursive reason to the demiurge's activities, it would be necessary to postulate a model for him to execute. The further implication is that the model or plan must not only be in (see "everything is in another" 12–13), but be identical to, the demiurge; in which case the demiurge would be Intellect and not discursive reason.

7, 13 *since nothing exists in-between*: I have taken this closely with the phrase that follows to indicate that all the elements of the universe described in the previous lines, which are described in a mode of creation that discursive thought makes discrete and temporally sequential, are, in the intelligible world, together with nothing between them.

7, 13–14 *because of the close neighborhood of all things to each other (*pros allo*) in real being (*onti*)*: I take this as referring to the internal structure of the intelligible world, as do Theiler and Armstrong. Laurent, however, understands "other (*allo*)" as referring to matter and "in" "in real being" in the weak sense of "in the case of being," to give the meaning: because of the closeness of true being to what is other than it (matter); thus the phrase explains "nothing in between" as meaning "between being and matter" (as the physical universe).

Laurent's interpretation, though perhaps more difficult to derive from the Greek, gives greater emphasis to the notion that there is an immediacy in the relationship of the intelligible and physical universe as expressed in the phrase "all at once, as it were, made manifest . . . facilitator." This observation of Plotinus is, in any case, an important corrective to the necessity (because of our recourse to discursive reason) of expressing the production of the universe in terms of "process" through a sequence of hypostases. See the remarks of Perl in his Introduction to V.1 in this series (16–18). This does not, however, mean that Plotinus has abandoned the distinctions he elsewhere makes, as we see from the remark that such distinctions are not relevant for "the present discussion." A similar suppression of distinctions between the One, Intellect, and Soul is apparent in the treatise on the *Presence of Being* (VI.4 and 5).

7, 22 *since matter too is a sort of ultimate form*: The description of matter as a kind of form is surprising in view of Plotinus' concern to remove all positive characteristics from matter (see particularly II.5.4 and III.6.13). Laurent plausibly suggests that Plotinus might be referring here to his view that although matter is "non-being" it is not "absolute non-being," that in identifying it as "privation" (*steresis*) rather than "something deprived of everything" it is a sort of "something" with a role to play and not a total non-entity. There is a sense in which the One and matter, at polar ends of his system, lie both beyond the normal range of Greek metaphysical concepts, and thus understandable that terminological approximations, such as calling matter a sort of form, are sometimes unavoidable. This idea also allows Plotinus to declare that the physical universe is entirely form, thus avoiding falling into the sort of gnostic dualism that entails the positing of a second primary principle. The origin of matter as "non-being" is clearly a problem for Plotinus, but he does seem to have accepted that it was ultimately a product of the One, even if through the medium of soul.

7, 24 *without noise*: See on 11, 6.

7, 26–27 *nothing to hinder*: Plotinus often maintains the effortless manner in which the world soul can fashion and control the world without hindrance. This distinguishes it from partial souls, since it is its universal and whole nature that enables its effortless control and its command over the stable totality (rather than the changing detailed parts) of the universe that prevents the world from being a hindrance to it. See I.8 [6] 2, 10–14: "In the All all parts are naturally set in their appropriate place—and our individual bodies need a great deal of troublesome thought, since many alien forces assail them and they are continually in the grip of poverty, and require every sort of help as being in great trouble." This idea goes back to Plato's *Timaeus*, where the difference between the situation of the individual soul and the world soul is due to the fact that the world body is perfect and stable as a whole (it loses nothing and gains nothing, *Timaeus* 33c6–7). The implication here is that the human body, as Plato says in *Timaeus* 81bff., does fluctuate and this fluctuation is the cause of passions, etc.

7, 28 *nothing is a hindrance to it*: See IV.3.10, 20f., where he explains that universal soul does not encounter hindrance in its creative forming of the universe. This occurs only later when the rational principle is operating at a micro level. "In the things that come after, one often hinders another and they are deprived of the attainment of their proper form, that which the formative principle operating on a small scale wishes them to have; but there in the universe as a whole, where the whole form is produced by soul and the things which are produced have all together an order, what has come into being is beautiful without labor or hindrance" (trans. Armstrong).

7, 28–35 This digression on the activity of the individual within the cosmic system well illustrates the important, though subordinate, nature of this topic to the main concern of this treatise with the universal. The injunction to live at the level of the world soul (and of the souls in the stars) even during our earthly life occurs again in II.9.2, 5 and 18, 30f. See Smith (2005, 66–67).

7, 32 *other than himself*: Identifying oneself with the lower level of the self is equated with the imposition of immanent form on the body to produce man. This is to be understood primarily as the embodiment of the soul, but since it is possible to transcend this level even during our earthly lives, the fall into body and becoming "man" may also be interpreted as an event in the spiritual life of the individual.

7, 33 *Man*: "Man" here is the intelligible form of man. See VI.7 [38], 2–6 for the difference between the transcendent form of Man and the immanent form of man in individuals.

When, however, Plotinus a few lines later refers to "ceasing to be man" he seems to be invoking the idea that the transcendent man is, in fact, more than man. Similarly in V.3.4, 11 he speaks of ceasing to be man in our ascent and union with Intellect. Elsewhere he speaks of becoming a god (I.2.7, 27: "Our goal is not to become good men—our goal is to become gods!"). There need be no contradiction here when we consider that the Form Man is, like every other intelligible, at once man and everything else.

7, 38 *had to be the way it is*: See above 6, 16 and note on 7, 1–12. It is false to argue from the observed reason for a thing being what it is to the necessity of it being so. Rather it is so because its cause has already determined it. The conclusion (the final cause) precedes the working out of its causal force in the thing produced. It is in this way that the conclusion may be said to precede the syllogism.

7, 43–44 *reasoning, demonstration, and conviction*: *logos, epideixis* and *pistis* are widely recognized Aristotelian terms for aspects of discursive reasoning. See VI.9.10, 5–6 for "knowledge which lies in demonstrations, convictions, and the reasoning of the soul."

7, 45 *it is well said*: The reference is to Aristotle *Physics* 188a27–30: "For first principles must not be derived from one another nor from anything else, while everything has to be derived from them." Aristotle is discussing the "principles" posited by his predecessors Anaxagoras, Empedocles,

Parmenides, and Democritus, who were right, according to Aristotle to make contraries such as hot/cold into principles since they are not derived from each other. Plotinus takes from this that a principle in the proper sense does not require any further cause. And this would be the case with Intellect because it contains within itself all its possible developments (its end). This need not conflict with the positing of the One as cause of Intellect, since the One is not strictly the cause of Intellect's totality, fullness, and variety (this is caused by Intellect itself), but only of its existence.

Chapter 8

The discussion now returns to the theme of beauty and the identification of beauty with the intelligible archetype, which has been the subject of the previous chapters.

8, 1–3 Strictly speaking, what is primarily beautiful is not beautiful but Beauty.

8, 4 *or none of it at all*: This may seem so obvious as to be superfluous, but Plotinus probably means that things in this world may sometimes possess beauty and then lose it. He may have in mind a passage from Diotima's speech in Plato's *Symposium* 211a2–5 where it is implied that things that display secondary beauty (i.e., not the total beauty of the Form of Beauty) are beautiful "in one part, but not in another, sometimes beautiful, sometimes not."

8, 5f. *For that which is prior*: The One is beyond beauty. Because the One is beyond beauty the first manifestation of beauty is the content of Intellect, the "form and object of vision," which Intellect sees in self-contemplation.

8, 7 In the passage of Plato (*Timaeus* 37c7–d1) to which Plotinus refers, the demiurge looks at the actual world he has created. By making the demiurge look at the model Plotinus interprets Plato in terms of his own theory of productive contemplation which is set out in III.8, the earlier part of this whole treatise, in which what is created is a byproduct of the creator's contemplation of himself and of his prior.

The interpretation of the myth of the origin of the world in *Timaeus* as expressed in temporal and physical terms ("something more familiar to ourselves") as a means of more easily communicating non-temporal and spatial metaphysical truths became standard amongst later Platonists.

8, 13 *unaware of what is happening to him*: A phrase perhaps prompted by Plato *Phaedrus* 250a7–b1: "and do not know what has happened to them by reason of their perception being dim," referring to the initial recognition by embodied souls of what they had experienced before embodiment. It is here ascribed to ourselves in the search for the intelligible world, which we so often fail to recognize even though unconsciously we are aware of its effects in the world. See also I.6.2, 2f. for the initial and unconscious response of the soul to beauty.

8, 23 *those who find fault with this world*: Plotinus probably has already in mind the Gnostics whom he attacks in the last part of the original whole treatise (II.9).

Chapter 9

A form of contemplative exercise is now recommended in which an apprehension of the physical cosmos as a unified whole is dematerialized so as to lead us to an intellectual (rather than simply discursive) grasp of the intelligible universe in all its beauty.

9, 1f. The exercise begins with our perception of this physical universe ("this world") by means of "discursive reason" (*dianoia*). We are then encouraged to remove from it all corporeal traces and to modify our own cognition accordingly, so that we come to an intuitive or intellectual grasp. This is in effect the intelligible model where "all is together and each is separate" (19–20). We then return to consider the physical universe (28 "this universe"), which we also may now, in the light of our vision of its intelligible source, declare to be great and beautiful.

Plotinus refers to a similar exercise in II.9.17, 4f., although the object of contemplation in this case is the world soul: "they should have stripped off this bodily nature in their thought [*dianoia*] and seen what remained, an intelligible [*noētē*] sphere embracing the form imposed upon the universe . . ." "Movement" and "rest" are also incorporated into the same vision. A similar experiment of conceptually removing all physical mass from a sphere is employed in VI.4.7, 22–29, for the different purpose of grasping the idea of the omnipresence of an incorporeal power (in this case light).

9, 3 *"all together"*: This phrase is taken from Anaxagoras (DK59 B1) and is frequently cited by Plotinus to designate the sort of interpenetrating unity in plurality of the intelligible world: I.1.8, 8 (of the relationship of the individual intellect to Intellect as whole); III.6.6, 23; V.3.15, 21; 17,10; V.9.6, 3–8; 7, 11; VI.5.5, 4; 6, 3; VI.6.7, 4; 7.33, 8 (and also of the lesser unity of soul IV.1.2, 44; 4.11, 27; VI.4.14, 4 and 6).

9, 5f. The essential components of the intelligible model (sun, stars, earth, sea, and living creatures) are all repeated here from Chapter 3 and 4, but whereas there the gods were emphasized more than humans as the contemplators, in Chapters 8 and 9 the focus is on the human rather than the divine contemplator.

9, 8 *luminous*: Light for Plotinus is in itself incorporeal and can act as a link between the transcendent and physical universes. The inclusion of light here takes up the idea of light introduced in Chapter 3, 5–6.

9, 11–12 *remove*: Note here the strong personal exhortation (see the concluding injunction of V.3.17, 38: "remove everything") and the subtle change of focus from the image of the universe to the adjustment of the self, from removing matter and spatial features from the universe to removing them from the self. For the importance of preparing the self see I.6.9, 7f. with the image of fashioning the statue within oneself.

9, 9–10 *moving . . . still*: By not excluding either of these two features we will more easily grasp the presence of the categories of "movement" and "rest," which are essential to the intelligible world (see on 4, 12).

9, 13 *smaller in mass*: He is aware of the danger in this exercise of simply reducing size rather than eliminating mass altogether.

The appeal to god here is suggested by the *Phaedrus* passage cited above and of course the demiurge of *Timaeus* as well at *Timaeus* 27c: "All men, Socrates, who have any degree of right feeling, at the beginning of every enterprise, whether small or great, always call upon god." But it is also a way of alluding to the immense difficulty of making the transition from discursive reason to intellection, a transition which he elsewhere describes as transcending one's status as man: "and by that intellect he thinks himself again, no longer as man but as having become altogether other" (V.3.4, 10–12). The phrase "may he come" even recalls the appearance of the One itself to the contemplator who awaits him (VI.7.34, 8–9). It is, perhaps, not surprising that Plotinus sometimes suggests that the transition to the level of Intellect is as demanding and extraordinary as our experience of the One. Plotinus invokes prayer before reaching out to the One in V.1.6, 9 and in IV.9.4, 6–7 in discussing the unity and plurality of souls.

The god who made the sphere: Is the demiurge (for Plotinus, Intellect), who "made" the sphere or intelligible model of the universe.

9, 15f. This description, though expressed in terms of the unity in the demiurgic god of the multiplicity of gods, uses the language and concepts applied frequently by Plotinus to the unity in multiplicity of the intelligible world, the gods being here virtually the same as intelligible forms. See, for example, V.9.8, 2–4: "Each individual Form is not other than Intellect, but each is Intellect. And Intellect as a whole is all the Forms, and each individual Form is an individual intellect."

9, 20f. It is not altogether clear in these lines whether Plotinus is referring to the intelligible world as a whole or to its "parts." I have taken them as referring throughout to the "parts," that is, the individual gods. Others (e.g., Theiler, Armstrong, Laurent) take a different view and refer at least *to de* in line 25 to the whole. My interpretation understands "nor does any have parts" (23) to refer to each rather than the whole. This then continues with "nor is each like a power"; and in line 25 I have taken *to de* to refer also to each part rather than to the whole and so have translated it as "each one." The conclusion that each part is infinite (lines 25–26) I take to be confirmed by the statement in 26–27: "And that god (i.e., the intelligible world as a whole) is so great that even his parts are infinite."

9, 33 *appear to burn*: He does not mean that burning, etc., are illusions, but rather that the power perceived by us in these physical activities is an image, and therefore on a lower level of reality than power in the intelligible world. The same idea lies behind the reference to "the false being of this universe" (line 43). For a full discussion of what he thinks is happening in the physical world of change see III.6.6, 33f. where, in developing his concept of matter as impassive, he asks how physical objects evidently impact on each other. This, he argues, is not due to matter but to the appearance of immanent forms which come and go, thus producing the effect of coming into being and passing away.

9, 36ff. A key idea: being and beauty are closely related. Note that existence (*to einai*) is in this passage equated with "being" (*ousia*). See I.6. Also "truth" is involved here (33).

Chapter 10

Plotinus continues the description begun in the previous chapter of how we attain a vision of the intelligible world. It is initially expressed in the mythical language of Plato's Phaedrus, *since he wants to present his personal vision of the intelligible as a true interpretation of Plato and more generally of the Greek theological tradition represented by Hesiod.*

10, 1 *For this reason*: Zeus as Soul, and thus directly and primarily responsible for the world and its beauty, is the first to turn back to Kronos (Intellect) to contemplate the beauty which he imports to the world—"this universe requires beauty brought in as an image" (9, 43).

10, 1–3 *although he is the most senior . . . the first*: The myth of the birth of Zeus from Kronos has already been introduced in III.8.11, 35–45 and is cited again in this treatise's Chapter 12; see note on 12, 3f. Here that myth is linked with the procession of the gods in *Phaedrus.* Zeus is the most senior (i.e., the first) of the gods to proceed from Intellect (Kronos) but also the first to revert in contemplation of his source.

10, 5 *risen high*: The image of the rising sun recalls the Good of Plato's *Republic* and the patient waiting of the contemplative for the appearance of Intellect (See V.5.8, 1–5) or the One. See note on 9, 13.

10, 7 A reminiscence of Plato *Republic* 515e8f., where the prisoner led from the cave is at first blinded by the sunlight of the world outside and cannot at first look directly at the sun itself.

10, 13 "Justice" and "moral probity" (*sophrosyne*) are mentioned in *Phaedrus* 247d6f.

10, 14–15 *not the kind which men experience*: For the radical difference between virtue in this world and "virtue" in the intelligible world, see I.3 *On Virtues.*

10, 16 *But [that beauty] over all . . . the final thing*: The subject of this sentence presents some difficulties. The Greek has just the feminine article, which could refer to *sophrosyne*; but it makes more sense to understand it (as does Schwyzer) as *he physis tou kalou* ("the nature of beauty") referring grammatically to "nature" (*physis* in line 13), but explicable in terms of "the beauty that remains over all" which Zeus sees "last of all" (lines 23–24). Beauty is the supreme "form" that orders and harmonizes the entire intelligible world, as it does the physical world. True being is in fact identical with Beauty, as he claims in I.6.5, 19–20: "What does "really exist" mean? That they are beautiful things."

10, 17 *final*: Again a reminiscence of the *Republic* passage cited in the note to line 7. The sun is the very last thing that the former prisoner sees.

10, 18–20 *souls which see everything there and are generated from everything so that they embrace everything themselves too from beginning to end*: Souls (in their disembodied state) have a vision of the whole intelligible world and are in fact a product of this world in its entirety ("are generated from everything"). They also retain, in the form of *logoi*, all that they have seen in their intelligible source, in different levels of intensity, from their disembodied state right down to their embodied existence ("from beginning to end").

10, 20–22 *And they are there. . . . they are not divided*: Behind this lies the idea that part of our soul remains undescended (see IV.8.8, 43; IV.7.13, 12–13). But it is also possible for the entire soul to be in touch with the intelligible world when we are freed from the physical limitations of our bodies. This freedom may be achieved not only after our physical death but also during our lifetime, if we live the philosophical life and manage to transcend our bodily concerns. This is the sort of life Plotinus describes elsewhere as living at the level of the world soul, when we may govern our bodies with ease, like the world soul. But it is not always clear when and to what extent we as individuals can be "entirely" present in the intelligible. Although this might seem to be reserved for those periods between re-embodiments, Plotinus sometimes, and more logically, suggests that the truly good man reaches this state even during earthly life. And since life at this level is timeless, the question of the duration of the experience is meaningful only in a relative sense, that is, in relation to his earthly time-based life. See II.9.2, 4ff. for the undescended part of the soul and the notion of effortlessly managing the body when engaged in contemplation beyond discursive reason. The late treatise I.4 [46] *On Well-Being* is particularly optimistic about the ability of the true philosopher to live at the intellectual level even in the most overwhelming physical circumstances. On this see Smith (1978).

10, 22 Individual souls are "divided" (*dieilēmmenai*) because they are present to specific bodies. The universal soul, however, is not so divided. See II.2.1, 40: "the whole soul is everywhere and, being the soul of the All, is not divided (*dieilēmmenē*) part to part."

10, 27 *sandy-red*: Plotinus seems to be referring to the reflection of light from the higher parts of the Nile Valley whose geological formation produced a sandy-red color. Cf. Said (1981, 370): "in the "Lower Pleistocene hyper-arid phase . . . 1.85 to 0.70 million years b.p. Egypt became desert, the Nile Valley became seismically active and wind action was at its maximum. It was interrupted by a short pluvial period resulting in the formation of gravel beds alternating with graded-sand or marl beds embedded in a yellow-red matrix and topped by a cemented red breccia."

10, 30 For Plotinus' theory of physical color see IV.5.7, 34–49. Color in this world is a product of the activity of light and appears on a surface as in a mirror but without penetrating its interior. This sort of color is excluded from being identified with true beauty earlier in this treatise (2, 8). But in the intelligible world "color" is of a different order and is found throughout the intelligible substance ("from its innermost depths"). This is another striking affirmation of Plotinus' positive engagement with the manifestations of physical beauty, since "color" would be totally excluded from the intelligible world, too, if Plato's statement that "being is colorless" (*Phaedrus* 247c, which Plotinus entertains in I.6.5, 10–11) were to be taken absolutely.

10, 39f. *But he must now bring it into himself*: The previous lines have described a stage of contemplation that is already beyond normal discursive reason, where the contemplator is already no longer a spectator and in which the difference between external and internal object of contemplation already seems to have been overcome, but in which the contemplator still regards what he sees within as being external. He must now proceed to the final state of reaching pure intellection, which is the subject of the following chapter.

Chapter 11

He now continues with the final point of the last chapter, the distinction between seeing the Beautiful and possessing it as identical with oneself. How is it possible to rise above the level of seeing the Intelligible as other than oneself. Plotinus here stresses the process of oscillation between reasoning about Intellect and identity with it, which precedes our full integration with it. In fact this full integration is not accompanied by our awareness of it, because it is the proper condition of our higher self, just as we are less aware of health (our proper condition) than illness. Our lack of "awareness" of our union with Intellect is an important theme of the very late treatise I.4.

11, 1ff. At the beginning of IV.8.1 *On the Descent of the Soul*, he describes this experience of transition between different levels of cognition and awareness: "I often wake up from my body into my true self, so that being within myself and outside all other things I enjoy a vision of wonderful beauty" (trans. Fleet). And in VI.5.7, 2–11 he stresses the essential feature of intellectual activity as identity of the thinker with the whole of intelligible reality: "we reach up to that level [Being] and the first thing that comes from it, and we think those objects without having images or impressions of them. But if we do not have images or impressions of them, we think them by being them. So if we participate in true knowledge, we are those objects, not by taking them into ourselves, but rather by ourselves being in them. But since others too, not only we, are those objects, all of us are those objects; and therefore since we are together, we are those objects with all, Thus we are all one. Yet since we look outward from the point where we are attached to them, we are unaware that we are one like faces that are on the outside many but have but a single head on the inside" (trans. Emilsson and Strange).

11, 3–4 *image of himself . . . into unity with himself*: Theiler takes the two pronouns here as non-reflexive, referring them to god. The same idea of inspecting the beauty of the inner self is found in I.6.9, 6f. but the stress here is on this as an image and therefore second best to the original which can only be found at a yet higher level. This looking at the self as an image of the self, and in this sense external, is the experience described at the end of the previous chapter. It is, perhaps, similar to the stage or type of self-knowledge described in V.3.5.1–19, a form of self-knowledge that still involves division compared with true self-knowledge: "but if it has them themselves [the objects of contemplation including the self] it does not see them as a result of dividing itself, but it was contemplator and possessor before it divided itself" (V.3.5, 19–21).

11, 6 *silently*: The realm of Intellect is frequently described as silent. It transcends the use of verbal descriptions and the structure of language that may be regarded as its discursive image. The word used here (*apsophēti*) also invokes a lack of disturbance, a feature of the comparison of health as our normal natural state with the experience of union with Intellect in lines 25f. Plotinus has possibly borrowed the word from Plato *Theaetetus* 144b6, who may in turn be borrowing it from some poetical source; it is rather a rare word.

11, 16 *with confidence (kata pistin)*: See 7, 44 for *pistis.* Plotinus understands *pistis* in the Aristotelian sense of rationally supported conviction, rather than in the Platonic sense of a rationally ungrounded belief. And so it designates in VI.7 an important cognitive stage in the ascent to Intellect and the One which both lie beyond discursive thought. See Smith (1992, 27–30).

11, 24 *by wanting to perceive too much*: For example, wanting to perceive that one is perceiving the intelligible. This absence of "awareness," referred to later when he says that "we have no perception of what belongs to us" is a positive state unlike the absence of awareness described in 8, 13 and 10, 37. But, as is made clear by the description of it in line 23 as "a sort of understanding or perception of itself" (*hoion synesis kai synaisthēsis*), it does not constitute a total and absolute lack of awareness, but rather the sort of super-awareness, analogous to the super-rationality of intellect that is above both rationality and irrationality. In fact it is the only true level of knowing, where knower and known are completely one. See Smith (1978).

11, 32 *our self-knowledge*: I have taken the possessive pronoun (*hēmōn*) as an objective genitive, "knowledge of ourselves."

11, 38–40 True self-knowledge can only be achieved by intellectual introspection. If at this level we do not accept this, we would be denying our own existence, an existence which it would be impossible, at this level, to affirm by perception. The term "perception" (*aisthēsis*) in these lines must refer not only to physical perception but to all acts of cognitive perception below the level of intellect. As at the beginning of V.5, the model of physical perception, which involves the notion of separation between observer and observed, is applicable also to mental perception at the level of discursive reason.

Chapter 12

The subject now turns to what in fact can be communicated to our discursive selves about our experience of unity with Intellect. This topic of the image we have of union with Intellect, or even with the One, constitutes the core of Plotinus' philosophizing about the nature of Intellect and the One. In this treatise, however, the stress is on the beauty and, therefore, the goodness of the universe as an image of its intelligible model rather than on the individual and his place in it. Moreover the affirmation of the beauty of the universe is interwoven with a mythological account of the structure of reality, thus continuing the mythological expression which is an important element of the treatise and which is intensified in the concluding chapter before he turns to the epistemological discussion of V.5.

12, 2 *whether as other or as remaining his true self*: These are the two final levels or stages of ascent to unity with Intellect that were discussed in the last two chapters. The term "other" (*heteros*) refers to the lower state; the phrases "by himself being it" (literally "as himself") and "as remaining his true self" (literally, "as having remained himself") refer to the higher state of union. I have expanded the last phrase to avoid the possible ambiguity of the literal translation, which could be interpreted to mean "by remaining on the level of himself, as opposed to becoming identical with intellect." But the description in 11, 4 of the man who contemplates at the very highest level as "coming into unity with himself" supports the notion that in the present context "being oneself" refers to the very highest aspect of the self, the true self, as opposed to the secondary self or empirical self.

12, 3f. Recent critics have tended to downplay Plotinus' use of myth, particularly of a theological kind. But his frequent employment of it cannot be ignored as a method of clarifying, as here, transcendent relationships that not even rational discourse can fully or adequately express. His treatise on Love (III.5), itself an extensive interpretation of Platonic myth, contains an important reflection on the value of myth (III.5.9, 24–29): "But myths, if, indeed, they are going to be myths, must separate temporally their narrative and divide from each other many Beings which exist together, but are distinct from each other by rank or powers, in the same way that rational accounts, too, produce generations for the ungenerated, that is, separating out what is together. And when they have instructed as best they can, they allow someone who has understood them to proceed to put together again what has been separated."

The myth of Ouranos, Kronos, and Zeus (cf. Hesiod *Theogony* 116f., 453f.), interpreted as representing the One, Intellect, and Soul, is introduced by Plotinus at key points in the combined treatise (III.8, V.8, V.5, II.9): III.8.11, 35–45; V.8.12–13; V.5.3, 16–24. See the analysis of Pierre Hadot (1981), who notes how Plotinus' reading of the myth suppresses the elements of catastrophe and violence, which are interpreted positively: the rebellion of Kronos against Ouranos and his mutilation become the necessary separation and origin of Intellect, Zeus' revenge and binding of Kronos becomes Kronos binding himself in the sense of containing himself within the intelligible world and not descending to the lower level, that of Soul, to which Zeus is assigned. This positive interpretation serves to differentiate his own benign view of the universe as a necessary and beautiful creation as opposed to the Gnostic view of the universe as a flawed entity, the calculated creation of a fallen deity. It seems not unlikely that this myth may have been used by Gnostics to this end, thus prompting Plotinus to deploy it in his dialogue with them, but with his own positive interpretation.

12, 4 *everything*: The whole intelligible world. But "*panta*" may be taken as masculine singular rather than neuter plural (so Theiler, Armstrong), in which case it means "in his entirety" referring to the child. But the plural seems more likely, as it is taken up again in lines 5–7, with its clear reference to both the unitary and multiple nature of the intelligible world.

12, 7–8 *more beautiful for remaining within*: The children of Kronos whom he swallowed are the Forms, which are more beautiful, as Forms with Intellect, than their less perfect images that are transmitted as *logoi* to Soul and the physical universe. The one exception is the hypostasis Soul (Zeus), which transmits the contents of Intellect to the universe. See also V.1.7, 30–37 for the similar interpretation of the same myth.

12, 12 *his other universe*: The exact meaning of "*autou*" (his) is not clear. Theiler takes it as reflexive and referring to Zeus (Soul), that is, this physical world is his world. Or it may refer to the Father of Zeus, Intellect, which seems the simplest solution. At any rate the world referred to here is the physical world.

12, 14 *it is not lawful*: The One and Being necessarily produce something other than themselves, not in the sense of their being compelled, but because it is their nature to produce in accord with their abundance of power.

12, 20 *they are wrong*: The Stoics (*SVF* I.98) held that the world would come to an end (although they argued that world history would be repeated again). But he more likely has the Gnostics in mind, for in II.9.4, 17 he implies, in the context of criticisms that the Gnostics taught that god created the world as if he planned it at a particular time, that their cosmogony would also involve the destruction of the universe. Even if this is a polemical interpretation of Gnostic views, it could justify Plotinus' insertion of this criticism here.

Chapter 13

The Hesiodic myth is further expanded here with greater emphasis on the metaphysical structuring of reality in which Ouranos, Kronos, and Zeus represent the One, Intellect, and Soul and the precise location of Beauty itself (the primary beauty) is reaffirmed as being in the intellectual realm both in the sense of universal Intellect and our own selves at the level of intellect.

13, 1 The "god who is bound" is Kronos, who is tied down in the sense that he "remains the same" because the intelligible world that he represents is always stable. His son is Zeus, representing Soul.

13, 4 *enough of beauties*: There can never be a surfeit of contemplation, and therefore of beauty, in the intelligible world. See 4, 27–36.

13, 5 *his own father*: That is Ouranos (the One). Kronos (Intellect) returns in contemplation toward the One. Plotinus is here referring to his own doctrine that the "as yet" unformed Intellect, by returning toward the One to contemplate it and take an impression from it ("established his own father in himself"), completes its formation of itself as Intellect.

13, 8 *otherness*: A term used by Plotinus particularly for the relationship of the Intellect to the One, for example in V.1.1, 4, where "the primary otherness" is the first manifestation of difference, being other (than total oneness), seen at the level of Intellect.

13, 9 *cut off*: Perhaps an allusion to Kronos castrating his father Ouranos although the verbal form with a negative is used frequently by Plotinus to represent the fact that lower hypostases are never cut off from their source.

bond: See on line 1 above.

13, 11 *too great to be designated beauty*: The One (Ouranos) is here clearly said to be above beauty, and Beauty itself is identified with Intellect (Kronos). Plotinus' insistence on the utter transcendence of the One frequently presented him with semantic difficulties when trying to express in causal terms the origin of specific characteristics, beginning with Intellect. He places Beauty at the level of Intellect in VI.2 [43] 18. but in VI.7 [38] 22 and 32 puts what he calls the "flower of beauty" beyond Intellect. In I.6.9, 39–43, he appears to hesitate at which level to ascribe it. See the note to I.6.9, 39–43 in this series and Smith (2004).

13, 15 There is no reason to regard the identification of Aphrodite here with soul as contradicting (so Armstrong) the earlier identification of soul with Zeus, if we take Aphrodite here as the soul of the universe (world soul) and Zeus as the hypostasis Soul. Plotinus here is deliberately ("to speak in more familiar terms") reverting to a more accessible concept (*gnōrimōteron*: literally "more easily recognized" or "known") of soul as the "soul of the universe." In so doing he also makes, by means of the world-soul, a closer link between Soul and the physical universe, whose basic beauty and goodness he has been concerned to uphold.

13, 19–22 In this grand penultimate "sentence" the conclusion that the origin of beauty is in the intelligible world is derived from the analysis of our own experience of attaining that level. This summarizes effectively the practical structure of this treatise in which he seeks to lead his audience to the true nature of beauty through the human capacity for discursive reasoning and, most importantly, of intellectual apprehension.

13, 24 The "other route" is the epistemological analysis of intellect, which is the subject of V.5.

Select Bibliography

I. Ancient Authors

ALCINOUS: *The Handbook of Platonism*, ed. and trans. Dillon, J. 1993. Oxford.

ALEXANDER OF APHRODISIAS: *Alexander Aphrodisiensis De anima libri mantissa*, ed. Sharples, R. W. 2008. Berlin: De Gruyter.

Alexander of Aphrodisias on the Soul: Part I, trans. Caston, V. 2012. London: Bristol Classical Press.

ANAXAGORAS: DK59 in Diels-Kranz. *Die Fragmente der Vorsokratiker*. 6th ed. Berlin: Weidmann, 1961.

APOLLONIUS RHODIUS: ed. Fränkel, H. 1961. Oxford.

ARISTOTLE: *Parts of Animals*, ed and trans. Peck, A. L. and E. S. Forster. 1937. London: Heinemann (Loeb).

Generation of Animals, ed. and trans. Peck, A. L. 1942. London: Heinemann (Loeb).

On Generation and Corruption in Loeb Aristotle vol. III, ed. and trans. Furley, D. J. 1955. London: Heinemann (Loeb).

Rhetoric, ed. and trans. Freese, J. H. 1926. London: Heinemann (Loeb).

Physics, ed. and trans. Wicksteed, P. H. and F. M. Cornford. 1957 London: Heinemann (Loeb).

CICERO: *On the Nature of the Gods*, ed. and trans. Rackham, H. 1933. London: Heinemann (Loeb).

DIO OF PRUSA: *Discourses* 12–13, ed. and trans. Cohoon, J. W. 1939. London: Heinemann (Loeb).

DIOGENES LAERTIUS: *Lives and Doctrines of the Philosophers*, ed. Long, H. S. 1964. Oxford.

HESIOD: *Theogony*, ed. and trans. Evelyn-White, H. G. 1936. London: Heinemann (Loeb).

HOMER: *Iliad*, ed. Munro, D. B. and Allen, T. W. 1920. Oxford: Clarendon Press.

LUCIAN: ed. and trans. Harmon, A. M. et al. 1921–1967. London: Heinemann (Loeb).

PHILO: *On the Creation of the World*, ed. and trans. Colson, F. H. and G. H. Whitaker. 1929. London: Heinemann (Loeb).

PHILOSTRATUS: *Life of Apollonius of Tyan*, ed. and trans. Conybeare, F. C. 1912. London: Heinemann (Loeb).

PLATO: *Opera*, ed. Burnet, J. 1900–1907. Oxford: Oxford University Press.

Collected Dialogues, trans. and ed. Hamilton, E. and H. Cairns. 1963. New York: Pantheon Books.

SENECA: *On Benefits*, in *Moral Essays*, Vol. III, ed. and trans. Basore, J. W. 1935. London: Heinemann (Loeb).

Letters, ed. and trans. Gummere, R. M. 1917. London: Heinemann (Loeb).

II. Editions and Translations of the *Enneads*

Armstrong, A. H. 1966–1982. *Plotinus, Enneads*. Greek Text with English Translation and Introductions. 7 vols. Cambridge, MA: Loeb.

Bréhier, Émile. 1924–1938. *Plotin, Ennéades*. Greek Text and French Translation with Introductions and Notes. 7 vols. Paris: Les Belles Lettres.

Cilento, Vincenzo. 1947–1949. *Plotino, Enneadi*. Italian Translation and Commentary. 3 vols. Bari: Laterza.

Creuzer, Georg Friedrich. 1835. *Plotini Enneades*. Greek Text, with Marsilio Ficino's Latin Translation and Commentary. Oxford: E Typographeo Academico.

Brisson, Luc and Jean François Pradeau, eds. 2002–2010. *Plotin Traités*. French Translation and Introductions. 8 vols. Paris: Flammarion.

Harder, Richard, Beutler, Robert, and Theiler, Willy. 1956–1971. *Plotins Schriften.* Greek Text with German Translation and Commentary. 12 vols. Hamburg: Meiner.

Henry, Paul and Schwyzer, Hans-Rudolph. 1951–1973. *Plotini Opera* I-III (editio maior). Paris: Desclée de Brouwer et Cie (HS_1).

Henry, Paul and Schwyzer, Hans-Rudolph. 1964–1982. *Plotini Opera* I-III (editio minor, with revised text). Oxford: Clarendon Press (HS_2).

Igal, Jesus. 1982–1998. *Plotino, Enéadas.* 3 vols. Introduction, translations and notes. Madrid: Gredos.

Kalligas, P. 2006. *Plotinus Ennead I* (in modern Greek). Athens: Akademia Athinon.

Laurent, J. 2002. In *Plotin. Traités 1–6,* eds. Brisson, L. and Pradeau, J.-F. Paris: Flammarion.

MacKenna, Stephen. 1962^3. *Plotinus: The Enneads.* English Translation. Revised by B. S. Page. London: Faber & Faber.

———. 1991. *Plotinus. The Enneads.* Selected Treatises Revised with Notes by John Dillon. London: Penguin.

Schwyzer, Hans-Rudolph. 1987. "Corrigenda ad Plotini Textum." *Museum Helveticum* 44, 181–210 (HS_5).

III. Studies on V.8 and Related Works

Anton, John P. 1964. "Plotinus' Refutation of Beauty as Symmetry," In JAAC XXIII: 233–237.

———. 1967. "Plotinus' Conception of the Functions of the Artist." In *The Journal of Aesthetics and Art Criticism* 26: 91–101.

Armstrong, A. H. 1961. "Platonic *Eros* and Christian *Agape.*" In *Downside Review* 79: 105–121. (*Plotinian and Christian Studies.* IX. London: Variorum 1979).

Beierwaltes, W. 1961. "Die Metaphysik des Lichtes in der Philosophie des Plotins. In *Zeitschrift für philosophische Forschung* XV: 334–362.

Blumenthal, H. J. 1971. *Plotinus' Psychology. His Doctrines of the Embodied Soul.* The Hague: Nijhoff.

———. 1972. "Plotinus' Psychology: Aristotle in the Service of Platonism." In *International Philosophical Quarterly* XII, 3: 340–364.

Hadot, P. 1957. "Etre, Vie, Pensée chez Plotin et avant Plotin." In *Les Sources de Plotin,* Vendoeuvres: Fondation Hardt, V: 105–141.

———. 1976 "Le mythe de Narcisse et son interpretation par Plotin." Reprinted in *Plotin, Porphyre.* Études néoplatoniciennes. 1999. Paris: les Belles Lettres, 225–266.

Lamberton, R. 1989. *Homer the Theologian*. Berkeley: University of California Press.

Long, A. A. and Sedley, David. 1987. *The Hellenistic Philosophers*, 2 vols. Cambridge: Cambridge University Press.

Miles, Margaret M. 1999. *Plotinus on Body and Beauty*. Oxford: Blackwell.

Said, Rushdi. 1962. *The Geology of Egypt*. Amsterdam and New York: Elsevier Publishing Company. Reprinted 1981.

Sedley, David. 1997. "'Becoming Like God' in the *Timaeus* and Aristotle," in *Interpreting the Timaeus-Critias*, eds. Calvo, T. and Brisson, L. Sankt Anton: Academia Verlag, 327–339.

———. 1999. "The Idea of Godlikeness" in *Oxford Readings in Philosophy. Plato 2*, ed. Fines, G. Oxford: Oxford University Press.

Sheppard, Anne. 1987. *Aesthetics. An Introduction to the Philosophy of Art*. Oxford: Oxford University Press.

Smith, A. 1974. *Porphyry's Place in the Neoplatonic Tradition*. The Hague: Nijhoff.

———. 1992. "Reason and Experience in Plotinus." Reprinted in *Plotinus, Porphyry and Iamblichus: Philosophy and Religion in Neoplatonism*. (2011) VI. London: Variorum.

———. 2011. "Image and Analogy in Plotinus." In *Proceedings of the Boston Area Colloquium in Ancient Philosophy* XXVII: 1–19.

———. 2014. "The Beauty of Divine Intellect in Plotinus." In *The Beauty of God's Presence in the Fathers of the Church* (ed. Rutherford, J. E.). Dublin: Four Courts Press.

Stamatellos, Giannis. 2007. *Plotinus and the Presocratics.* Albany: State University of New York Press.

Wilberding, James. 2006. *Plotinus' Cosmology: A Study of Ennead II.1 (40).* Oxford: Oxford University Press.

IV. General Publications

Alt, K. 1993. *Weltflucht und Weltbejahung. Zur Frage des Leib-Seele Dualismus bei Plutarch, Numenius, Plotin.* Stuttgart: Franz Steiner Verlag.

Armstrong, A. H. 1966–1982. *The Architecture of the Intelligible Universe in the Philosophy of Plotinus.* Cambridge: Cambridge University Press.

Armstrong, A. H., ed. 1967. *The Cambridge History of Later Greek and Early Medieval Philosophy.* Cambridge: Cambridge University Press.

Arnou, R. 1968. *Le Désir de Dieu dans la philosophie de Plotin.* 2nd ed. Rome: Presses de l'Université Grégorienne.

Dillon, J. 1977/1996. *The Middle Platonists: A Study of Platonism, 80 B.C.–A.D. 220*, London: Duckworth, 1977, 1996².

Dodds, Eric R. 1965. *Pagan and Christian in an Age of Anxiety: Some Aspects of Religious Experience from Marcus Aurelius to Constantine*. Cambridge: Cambridge University Press.

Emilsson, E. K. 1988. *Plotinus on Sense-Perception.* Cambridge: Cambridge University Press.

———. 2007. *Plotinus on Intellect.* Oxford: The Clarendon Press.

Gatti, M. L. 1996. *Plotino e la metafisica della contemplazione.* Milan: Vita e Pensiero.

Gerson, L. P. 1994. *Plotinus.* London/New York: Routledge.

———, ed. 1996. *The Cambridge Companion to Plotinus.* Cambridge: Cambridge University Press.

———, ed. 2010. *The Cambridge History of Philosophy in Late Antiquity.* 2 vols. Cambridge: Cambridge University Press.

Guthrie, W. K. C. 1967–1978. *A History of Greek Philosophy*, 5 vols. Cambridge: Cambridge University Press.

Hadot, Pierre. 1993. *Plotinus on the Simplicity of Vision.* Translated by M. Chase. Chicago: Chicago University Press.

Inge, W. R. 1948. *The Philosophy of Plotinus.* 3rd ed. London: Longmans, Green.

Les Sources de Plotin. 1960. Entretiens Fondation Hardt V. Vandoeuvres-Genève.

Lloyd, Anthony C. 1990. *The Anatomy of Neoplatonism.* Oxford: Clarendon Press.

O'Daly, G. 1973. *Plotinus' Philosophy of the Self.* Shannon: Irish University Press.

O'Meara, Dominic J. 1993. *Plotinus: an Introduction to the Enneads.* Oxford: Oxford University Press.

Pépin, J. 1958. *Mythe et allégorie: les origins grecques et les contestations judéo-chrétiennes.* Paris: Aubier.

Remes, Pauliina. 2007. *Plotinus on Self: The Philosophy of the 'We.'* Cambridge: Cambridge University Press.

Remes, Pauliina. 2008. *Neoplatonism.* Berkeley: University of California Press.

Rist, John M. 1967. *Plotinus: The Road to Reality.* Cambridge: Cambridge University Press.

Schniewind, Alexandrine. 2003. *L'Éthique du Sage chez Plotin.* Paris: J. Vrin.

Smith, A. 2004. *Philosophy in Late Antiquity.* London: Routledge.

Wallis, R. T. 1995. *Neoplatonism.* 2nd ed. London: Duckworth.

West, M. L. 1966. *Hesiod* Theogony, *Edited with Prolegomena and Commentary.* Oxford: Clarendon Press.

Index of Ancient Authors

ALCINOUS

The Handbook of Platonism

163, 21–23 76

ANAXAGORAS

Fr. B1 120

Fr. B11 93

APOLLONIUS RHODIUS

I.151–5 95

ARISTOTLE

On Generation and Corruption

328a15 95

Generation of Animals

729a32 78

Metaphysics

1071b12–23 85

1074b15ff. 85

Parts of Animals

651a14–15 78

Physics

188a27–30 114

Rhetoric

1385b21 103

CICERO

On the Nature of the Gods

II.153 89

Orator

2.8–3.9 28

2.8–10 75

DIO OF PRUSA

Orations

12 28

DIOGENES LAERTIUS

Lives of the Philosophers

IV.1 71

HESIOD

Theogony

116f. 137

453f. 137

HOMER

Iliad

6.138 91

LUCIAN

Gallus

20 103

PHILO

On the Creation of the World

54 89

PHILOSTRATUS

Life of Apollonius

VI.19.2 76

PLATO

Letters

VII 344a1 95

Phaedo

111a3 52

Phaedrus

246c1–2 57

246c7–d1 88

246e4–6 62

247f. 24, 87

247c 129

247c3–5 70

247c5–6 92

247c6–7 79

247c7 92

247c8 102

247d 91

247d6f. 126

247d7 50

247d7–e1 53

248a1 62

248a6–b5 95

248b6 92

248d3 96

249a1–2 96

249c4 96

249e4 62

250a7–b1 118

250b5–6 24

264e4–6 39

Philebus

35b 95

Republic

507b 103

508bf. 85

508c1 68

509a6 49, 102

509b 103

509b9 70

515e8f. 126

516e8 64
517b5 68
517c4 102
596a–599a 27
597bf. 75
597c3 73
597e 27
598a 27

Sophist
258f. 93

Symposium
203b5 63
211a2–5 117
215bf. 81
215b1–3 103
216e6–217a1 103
218e1 49
218e2 88

Theaetetus
144b6 133

Timaeus
27c 121
33c6–7 112
37c–d1 38
37c7–d1 58, 118

PLOTINUS
I.1.8, 8 120
I.2.1, 43–45 109
I.2.7, 27 114
I.3 126
I.3.4, 10–12 91
I.4 128, 131
I.6 21, 22, 27, 70
I.6.1, 20f. 78
I.6.2, 2f. 118
I.6.5, 10–11 129
I.6.5, 19–20 126
I.6.8, 8–12 81
I.6.9, 6f. 132
I.6.9, 7f. 121
I.6.9, 29f. 81
I.6.9, 39–43 140
I.8.2, 10–14 112
I.8.8, 6 95
II.2.1, 40 128
II.4.5, 7–8 85
II.4.13–14 74
II.5.4 111
II.6 94
II.9 17, 18, 118, 137
II.9.2, 4f. 128
II.9.2, 5 113
II.9.4, 17 138
II.9.5, 4–14 79
II.9.6, 43–52 75
II.9.17, 4f. 119
II.9.18, 30f. 89, 113
III.2.14, 25–30 79
III.5 136

III.5.6, 21–23 88
III.5.9 21, 95
III.5.9, 24–29 136
III.6.6, 23 120
III.6.6, 33f. 123
III.6.13 111
III.7.4, 1–8 92
III.8 17, 18, 19, 78, 81, 96, 118, 137
III.8.8, 17 96
III.8.10–11 69
III.8.10, 22 69
III.8.11 24
III.8.11, 26f. 70
III.8.11, 35–45 125, 137
III.8.12 70
IV.1.2, 44 120
IV.3.10, 20f. 112
IV.3.20, 25 79
IV.4.11, 27 120
IV.5.7, 34–49 129
IV.7.13, 12–13 127
IV.8.1 131
IV.8.8, 43 127
IV.9.4, 6–7 122
IV.9.5, 18 89
V.1.1 82
V.1.1, 4 140
V.1.6, 9 122
V.1.7, 30–37 138
V.1.8, 10–14 75, 97
V.3.4, 10–12 121
V.3.4, 11 114
V.3.5, 1–19 132
V.3.5, 19–21 133
V.3.5, 41–44 86
V.3.15, 21 120
V.3.17, 10 120
V.3.17, 38 120
V.5 17, 18, 19, 22, 24, 25, 70, 134, 135, 137, 141
V.5.1 68
V.5.1–2 92, 102
V.5.3, 16–24 137
V.8 17, 18, 19, 137
V.8.1, 1f. 24
V.8.1, 4–5 18
V.8.1, 13–14 77
V.8.1, 24 83
V.8.1, 36 83
V.8.1, 36–37 27
V.8.2 25
V.8.2, 17 83
V.8.3 25, 120
V.8.3, 3–4 80
V.8.3, 5–6 120
V.8.3, 11f. 71
V.8.3, 17f. 23
V.8.3, 20f. 92
V.8.4 26, 76, 77, 120

V.8.4–5 26
V.8.4, 10f. 22
V.8.4, 18–19 106
V.8.4, 27–36 139
V.8.4, 38 100
V.8.5, 1–5 126
V.8.5, 22–23 105
V.8.6 26, 71
V.8.6, 16 114
V.8.7 26
V.8.7, 1–2 114
V.8.7, 28–35 84, 88
V.8.7, 44 133
V.8.8 26, 120
V.8.8, 13 133
V.8.9 22, 26, 107, 120
V.8.9, 11–12 22
V.8.9, 35–42 74
V.8.10 26
V.8.10, 20–22 84
V.8.10, 37 133
V.8.10–13 26
V.8.11 26
V.8.11, 4 136
V.8.11, 6 112
V.8.12 26
V.8.12–13 137
V.8.12, 3f. 71, 125
V.8.13 26
V.9.1, 10–16 101
V.9.5 73
V.9.6, 3f. 89, 118
V.9.7, 11 120
V.9.8, 2–4 122
V.9.8, 8f. 103
VI.1–3 94
VI.2.7, 40 70
VI.2.18 140
VI.4–5 111
VI.4.7, 22–29 120
VI.4.14, 4 120
VI.4.14, 6 120
VI.4.16, 4–7 75
VI.5.5, 4 120
VI.5.6, 3 120
VI.5.7, 2–11 131
VI.6.6, 8–10 102
VI.6.7, 4 120
VI.7 133
VI.7.9, 40–46 76
VI.7.10, 24–28 78
VI.7.22 140
VI.7.32 140
VI.7.33, 1–7 97
VI.7.33, 8 120
VI.7.34, 8–9 121
VI.8.3, 13 95
VI.9.10, 5–6 114

Porphyry

Life of Plotinus

16 18

Seneca

On Benefits

I.3 71

Letters

65.7–10 75

65.8 28

Stoics

SVF

I.98 138

Index of Names and Subjects

Alcibiades 81, 103
analogy 86–87
Anaxagoras 89, 93, 114
Antiochus 28
Aphrodite 46, 68, 140
Aristotle 28, 81
Armstrong, A. H. 75, 79, 110, 113, 122, 137, 140
art 27f., 73, 75
artist 25, 76, 100
Beierwaltes 85
Chryippus 71
contemplation 18, 20, 23, 95
Democritus 115
demiurge 20
Diotima 117
Egypt 54, 128
color 129
Empedocles 114
Epictetus 81
epitēdeiotēs 72, 74

genera, five 93
Fleet, B. 131
Good, the 70, 85, 87, 126
Gnostics 18, 19, 20, 21, 89, 118, 137, 138
Gods 88
Graces 43, 72
Hadot, P. 137
Helen 45
Hesiod 19, 21, 26
Iamblichus 20
Intellect 18, 19, 23, 29
imitation 27f., 75
Kronos 19, 40, 68, 123, 137, 138, 139, 140
Laurent 79, 110, 122
light 85, 92, 120
logos 72, 77, 83
Lynceus 51, 95
Matter 25, 74, 110f.
muses 43, 63, 72
myth 19, 20, 21, 26, 71, 77, 136f.
Narcissus 81
nature 81
Nile 128
Olympia 28
One, the 18, 117
Ouranos 19, 40, 68, 137, 139, 140
Parmenides 115
Penia 96
Perl, E. 111
Pheidias 28, 45, 79
Phoebus 63

Plato 20, 23, 24, 28, 97
Phaedrus 20, 21, 26, 27, 77, 125
Republic 28, 87, 126
Symposium 27
Timaeus 21
Poros 96
Porphyry 17, 18, 20, 21
privation 111
Proclus 20
Pythagoras 81
Rist, J. 75
Said, R. 128
Smith, A. 85, 87, 113, 128, 140
Socrates 81, 88, 103, 121
soul 19
undescended 84, 127
world soul 84
Speusippus 72
Stamatellos 93
Stoics 28, 96, 101
Theiler, W. 76, 110, 122, 132, 137, 138
truth 70, 91f., 102, 123
wisdom 96f.
Zeus 19, 28, 40, 45, 52, 61, 62, 66, 79, 125, 126, 137, 139, 140

• ALSO AVAILABLE FROM PARMENIDES PUBLISHING •

PRE-SOCRATICS

By Being, It Is: *The Thesis of Parmenides* by Néstor-Luis Cordero

The Fragments of *Parmenides*: *A Critical Text with Introduction and Translation, the Ancient Testimonia and a Commentary by A. H. Coxon. Revised and Expanded Edition edited with new Translations by Richard McKirahan and a new Preface* by Malcolm Schofield

The Legacy of Parmenides: *Eleatic Monism and Later Presocratic Thought* by Patricia Curd

Parmenides and the History of Dialectic: *Three Essays* by Scott Austin

Parmenides, Venerable and Awesome: *Proceedings of the International Symposium* edited by Néstor-Luis Cordero

Presocratics and Plato: *A Festschrift in Honor of Charles Kahn* edited by Richard Patterson, Vassilis Karasmanis, and Arnold Hermann

The Route of Parmenides: *Revised and Expanded Edition, With a New Introduction, Three Supplemental Essays, and an Essay* by Gregory Vlastos by Alexander P. D. Mourelatos

To Think Like God: *Pythagoras and Parmenides. The Origins of Philosophy. Scholarly and fully annotated edition* by Arnold Hermann

The Illustrated To Think Like God: *Pythagoras and Parmenides. The Origins of Philosophy* by Arnold Hermann (with over 200 full color illustrations)

PLATO

A Stranger's Knowledge: *Statesmanship, Philosophy, and Law in Plato's Statesman* by Xavier Márquez

God and Forms in Plato by Richard D. Mohr

Image and Paradigm in Plato's Sophist by David Ambuel

Imperial Plato: Albinus, Maximus, Apuleius by Ryan Fowler

Interpreting Plato's Dialogues by J. Angelo Corlett

One Book, the Whole Universe: *Plato's Timaeus Today* edited by Richard D. Mohr and Barbara M. Sattler

Platonic Patterns: *A Collection of Studies* by Holger Thesleff

Plato's Late Ontology: *A Riddle Resolved* by Kenneth M. Sayre

Plato's Parmenides: *Text, Translation & Introductory Essay* by Arnold Hermann. Translation in collaboration with Sylvana Chrysakopoulou with a Foreword by Douglas Hedley

Plato's Universe by Gregory Vlastos

The Philosopher in Plato's Statesman by Mitchell Miller

ARISTOTLE

Aristotle's Empiricism: Experience and Mechanics in the Fourth Century B.C. by Jean De Groot

One and Many in Aristotle's Metaphysics—*Volume I: Books Alpha-Delta* by Edward C. Halper

One and Many in Aristotle's Metaphysics—*Volume 2: The Central Books* by Edward C. Halper

Reading Aristotle: Physics VII.3 "What is Alteration?" *Proceedings of the International ESAP-HYELE Conference* edited by Stefano Maso, Carlo Natali, and Gerhard Seel

HELLENISTIC PHILOSOPHY

A Life Worthy of the Gods: *The Materialist Psychology of Epicurus* by David Konstan

THE *ENNEADS* OF PLOTINUS

Translations with Introductions & Philosophical Commentaries
Series edited by John M. Dillon and Andrew Smith

Ennead I.1: ***What Is the Living Thing? What Is Man?*** by Gerard O'Daly

Ennead I.6: ***On Beauty*** by Andrew Smith

Ennead II.5: ***On What Is Potentially and What Actually*** by Cinzia Arruzza

Ennead II.9: ***Against the Gnostics*** by Sebastian Ramon Philipp Gertz

Ennead IV.3–IV.4.29: ***Problems concerning the Soul*** by John M. Dillon and H. J. Blumenthal

Ennead IV.4.30–45 & IV.5: ***Problems concerning the Soul*** by Gary M. Gurtler

Ennead IV.7: ***On the Immortality of the Soul*** by Barrie Fleet

Ennead IV.8: ***On the Descent of the Soul into Bodies*** by Barrie Fleet

Ennead V.1: ***On the Three Primary Levels of Reality*** by Eric D. Perl

Ennead V.5: ***That the Intelligibles are not External to the Intellect, and on the Good*** by Lloyd P. Gerson

Ennead VI.4 & VI.5: ***On the Presence of Being, One and the Same, Everywhere as a Whole*** by Eyjólfur Emilsson and Steven Strange

Ennead VI.8: ***On the Voluntary and on the Free Will of the One*** by Kevin Corrigan and John D. Turner

ETHICS

Sentience and Sensibility: *A Conversation about Moral Philosophy* by Matthew R. Silliman

PHILOSOPHICAL FICTION

Pythagorean Crimes by Tefcros Michaelides

The Aristotle Quest: A Dana McCarter Trilogy. Book 1: Black Market Truth by Sharon M. Kaye

AUDIOBOOKS

The Iliad (unabridged) by Stanley Lombardo

The Odyssey (unabridged) by Stanley Lombardo

The Essential Homer by Stanley Lombardo

The Essential Iliad by Stanley Lombardo

FORTHCOMING

Ennead* I.2: *On Virtues by Suzanne Stern-Gillet

Ennead* I.3: *On Dialectic by Pauliina Remes

Ennead* I.4: *On Well-Being by Kieran McGroarty

Ennead* I.5: *On Whether Well Being Increases With Time by Danielle A. Layne

Ennead* I.8: *On the Nature and Source of Evil by Anne Sheppard

Ennead* II.4: *On Matter by Anthony A. Long

Ennead* II.7: *On Complete Blending by Robert Goulding

Ennead* II.8: *On Sight by Robert Goulding

Ennead* III.4: *On Our Allotted Guardian Spirit by Wiebke-Marie Stock

Ennead* III.5: *On Love by Sara Magrin

Ennead* III.6: *On Impassibility by Eleni Perdikouri

Ennead* III.7: *On Eternity and Time by László Bene

Ennead* III.8: *On Nature and Contemplation by George Karamanolis

Ennead* IV.6: *On Sense-Perception and Memory by Peter Lautner

Ennead* V.2, V.4, and V.6: *On the One and Intellect by Eleni Perdikouri

Ennead* V.3: *On the Knowing Hypostases by Marie-Élise Zovko

Ennead* V.9: *On Intellect, Ideas, and Being by Matthias Vorwerk

Ennead* VI.1-2: *On the Genera of Being (I+II) by Damien Caluori and Regina Füchslin

Ennead* VI.3: *On the Genera of Being (III) by Riccardo Chiaradonna

Ennead* VI.7: *The Forms and the Good by Nicholas Banner

Ennead* VI.9: *On the Good or the One by Stephen R. L. Clark